the

cookbook

the

Peanut Butter & Co.

cookbook

recipes from the world's
nuttiest sandwich shop

by **lee zalben** • foreword by **jerry seinfeld**

photography by **theresa raffetto**

QUIRK BOOKS

PHILADELPHIA

For my mom, who always told me,
"If you can dream it, you can do it."

Library of Congress Cataloging-in-Publication Number: 2005921836

ISBN-10: 1-59474-056-9

ISBN-13: 978-1-59474-056-5

Printed in China

Typeset in Clarendon and Meta

Designed by Andrea Stephany

Photography by Theresa Raffetto
Food styling by Victoria Granof
Prop styling by Barbara Fritz

Distributed in North America by Chronicle Books
85 Second Street
San Francisco, CA 94105

10 9 8 7 6 5 4 3 2

Quirk Books
215 Church Street
Philadelphia, PA 19106
www.quirkbooks.com

contents

Foreword
by Jerry Seinfeld • "The Comedy Special"

IN MY EARLY DAYS OF STAND-UP COMEDY I lived in a tiny one-room apartment on the Upper West Side of Manhattan. It was called a "studio" but there was very little studying or painting going on in these miniscule rectangles. I had a sink the size of a deck of cards, and if someone wanted to burglarize the apartment they could just literally punch their fist through the wall, reach in, and take anything they wanted. It sounds like a joke, but I actually had that happen. But I loved the little place anyway.

And it was there, in an effort to feed myself with a minimum of time and money, that I invented a taste sensation I called "The Comedy Special." And because I like you and trust you, I am going to divulge here for the first time how you can make a Comedy Special for yourself just as I did in the late 1970s.

I lived near a famous New York bagel place called H&H. These are the greatest bagels in the world, and I'd be more than happy to punch the face of anyone who disagrees. They're so great I have not moved from this neighborhood for twenty-eight years. This is also the bagel place that was featured in the "Festivus" episode of my TV series, where we learned that Kramer was actually never unemployed but merely on strike from H&H Bagels for the entire nine years.

Anyway, back to the recipe. If you can't get an H&H, get the best bagel you can find. I prefer plain. There's nothing plain about plain. They only call them plain because the word "quintessential" is too cumbersome for the counter people who just want to keep the line moving.

Alright, so you take the bagel, slice it, toast it, then spread the best peanut butter in the world on it, which is from Peanut Butter & Co. in Greenwich Village. Again, I recommend the plain; don't let Lee Zalben talk you into any of the Frankensteinian variations on his all-time classic. I admit they're all excellent, but it's 1976, you're a young stand-up comic, you're broke, you're hungry, and this is no time for cuisine.

Okay, so you take the peanut butter, you spread it on the bagel halves, then take some honey, crisscross it in an Entenmann's Coffee Ring pattern as best you can on top of the now melting peanut butter. Then, sprinkle some cinnamon on top of that! Take your knife, shmush it all around a little bit—the cinnamon turns all dark, the peanut butter's pouring over the sides—pick it up while it's still warm, shove it in your face, and make a giant mess.

Peanut butter is scientifically proven to contain a chemical that is a natural antidepressant, which you're going to need as you head out to face a New York nightclub audience with some very shaky material.

Anyway, there you have it: Jerry Seinfeld's "Comedy Special" revealed here for the first time. If you can't get this right, go over to Lee's joint on Sullivan Street and he'll fix you right up with one of his amazing sandwiches, which I admit are delicious, just not very funny.

Introduction

When people meet me, one of the first questions they ask is, "Did you like peanut butter as a kid?" Of course I did! Who didn't? But in my house, peanut butter was something of an obsession. My mother, tired of opening the jar of peanut butter to see the outline of her two sons' fingers in the jar, kept three jars in the house at all times, labeled "Mom," "Lee," and "Scott" (my brother), so that we could "stick our fingers in to our heart's content with no fear of double-dipping." So I guess you could say I've been a peanut butter fan since way back when.

Peanut Butter & Co. started out as a crazy idea I had in college. During midterms and finals, my friends and I would have late-night study breaks where we would raid the cupboards of our small campus apartment and pull out all sorts of stuff to eat with our peanut butter and bread—dried apricots, chocolate chips, mini marshmallows, bananas; if it was there, we tried it. We had contests to see who could come up with the craziest but best-tasting sandwich. I always won, and I thought, "Wouldn't it be great if there was a place you could go and order any kind of peanut butter sandwich you could dream up?"

After graduation, I moved to New York City to begin a career in advertising. But I was an entrepreneur at heart, and I yearned to strike out on my own. One blustery Saturday in March of 1998 I was walking in Greenwich Village when I came across a vacant storefront near NYU and SoHo, just a few blocks from Washington Square Park and the West Third Street basketball courts. It struck me that this would be the perfect place for that peanut butter sandwich shop I dreamed about in college! I went to sleep that night and couldn't get the idea out of my head.

I spent the following day coming up with sandwich ideas and names for the shop. I couldn't concentrate at all at work on Monday, so I called the real estate agent to find out how much the rent was, just for kicks. The agent offered to show me the property the following morning on my way to work, and I took him up on the offer. The space was rough—it had been split in two and was a combination Japanese restaurant/reggae bar that needed to be completely refurbished. It would be a lot of work. But something inside me clicked, and I knew that I had found my destiny.

The following day I quit my job and took some freelance work while I wrote a business plan and learned everything I could about peanuts, peanut butter, and opening a restaurant. I met with suppliers and other restaurant owners to learn about the business. I invited friends over and whipped up peanut butter sandwiches and desserts for them to taste and critique.

By December of that year, we were two months behind schedule and 50 percent over budget, and the place still wasn't ready. I realized that we just had to open or it was never going to happen. Most of the equipment and supplies were in, but getting the contractors to finish the job was taking forever. I got everyone on the phone and told them that we were opening the following week, and if they couldn't finish in time, I would find someone who could.

On December 21, 1998, at 11:00 AM, we opened our doors to the public for the first time. The paint was barely dry when the first customers walked in the door. The first two sandwiches ordered at the shop were the last two sandwiches I thought anyone would ever want—an Elvis with bacon and a Peanut Butter BLT. We were still waiting for the grill to be installed, and we had only one propane burner and a single frying pan in the kitchen—those poor people had to wait a long time for their sandwiches! During the first few days, it seemed that everything went wrong all of the time, but we learned fast and quickly found a rhythm.

My favorite memory of the shop occurred a few weeks after we opened. Both the *New York Times* and *Time Out New York* had just published very nice reviews about us. We were hoping for a busy weekend, but as luck would have it, my best sandwich maker quit without notice, leaving us shorthanded in the kitchen. My mom volunteered to come up from Philadelphia to help out for a few days until I was able to hire someone new.

Well, we soon found out just how many people paid attention to the *New York Times* and *Time Out New York*. By one o'clock on Saturday people were lined up around the block waiting to come in. We had more business than we could handle. The tiny shop was filled with foodies, urban hipsters, local celebrities—people who could really influence our success or failure. The busboy couldn't wash the dishes fast enough. It was taking 30 to 40 minutes to get orders out, and my poor mother was in the back working as fast as she could. I'd run in the back to help with a few orders, but I'd inevitably be dragged back into the front to deal with impatient customers.

I could feel the tension in the room mounting and knew something had to be done. I stood on a chair and tapped a spoon on a glass to get everyone's attention. "Thank you all for coming to my little sandwich shop today," I said. "I know that some of you had to wait in line outside in the cold just to be seated, and that some of you have been waiting for more than half an hour for a peanut butter sandwich, which probably seems seem kind of silly." A few people chuckled. "We are obviously working out some of the kinks in the kitchen, but I want you to know that it's my own mother who's preparing your lunch for you today, and we are working as fast as we can. If you'll just hang in there a little longer, we'll get your food right out to you."

Everyone in the shop started clapping and cheering. Somebody yelled, "Yay Mom!" My mom poked her head out of the kitchen door, and they clapped even louder. I walked over to her and pulled her out, and they gave her a standing ovation. She took a little bow. I had never seen anything like it in my life, and at that moment I knew two things—first, that Peanut Butter & Co. was going to be bigger than I had ever imagined, and second, that I had the greatest mom in the whole wide world.

Since we opened our doors in 1998, Peanut Butter & Co. has become much more than just a place to get a good peanut butter sandwich. A few weeks after we opened, our customers started bringing in Tupperware containers—they'd say, "Great sandwich, Lee, but can I take home some of that dark chocolate peanut butter?" We started selling our peanut butter in our shop, and then on our Web site, www.ilove peanutbutter.com, shipping it all over the United States.

Then Dean & DeLuca, a specialty food store in New York, wanted to carry our peanut butter. At first we declined, because we didn't think we could make enough in our tiny little kitchen. But they wouldn't take no for an answer, so we gave in and sent a few cases of peanut butter for them to sell in their shop. We thought it would stop there, but there are a lot of gourmet food stores in New York, and they all started calling to get our peanut butter on their shelves. We couldn't keep up with the demand, so we built a little peanut butter factory in Brooklyn. Now our peanut butter is available at gourmet food shops, natural food stores, and better supermarkets across the United States.

Expanding our business to reach customers across the country has been a lot of work, but it's been lots of fun, too. I've spent many weekends giving out samples, and I love to meet our customers and hear about their favorite ways to eat our peanut butter.

The Peanut Butter & Co. Cookbook is all about finding fun new ways to eat peanut butter. Most of us have eaten peanut butter sandwiches all of our lives. I hope that this book will help you find new ways to make America's favorite spread part of your everyday life.

We look forward to bringing you the most delicious peanut butter in the world!

Lee Zalben, "The Peanut Butter Guy"
Peanut Butter & Co. Founder and President

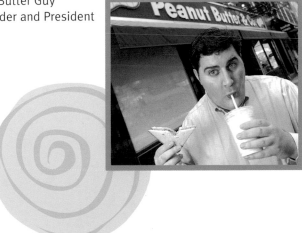

Peanut Butter Basics

The recipes in this book call for different varieties of Peanut Butter & Co. brand peanut butter, which we created in our Greenwich Village sandwich shop and now produce in our little peanut butter factory in Brooklyn. Our peanut butter is available at gourmet food stores, health food shops, and better supermarkets throughout the country, as well as on our Web site, www.ilovepeanutbutter.com. A list of stores where you can find our peanut butter appears in the Resources section on page 106.

While we recommend using our brand of peanut butter, you can substitute any all-natural salted peanut butter with no sugar added, or try making your own. If you use unsalted peanut butter, you may have to add salt to the recipe.

Making Your Own Peanut Butter

If you want to try making your own peanut butter, you'll need to know a little something about peanuts before you start.

There are four different kinds of peanuts grown in the United States: Virginia, Spanish, Runner, and Valencia. Each variety of peanut is grown in a different area of the country and is well-suited for a different purpose. Just as the grapes that are used to make wine are not the same as those used in a fruit salad, peanuts for snacking and peanuts for peanut butter are different varieties.

Virginia and Valencia peanuts are great for snacking, but for the best-tasting peanut butter use the Runner and Spanish varieties, as they retain the most flavor and the best texture after they've been ground. In fact, most peanut butter in the United States is made from Runner peanuts.

When choosing peanuts to make peanut butter, you also have to think about the roast. Just as the length of time that raw coffee beans are roasted will affect the color and flavor of your morning brew, the longer the peanuts are roasted, the darker the color and flavor of both the peanut and the resulting peanut butter.

Always use unsalted peanuts when making peanut butter so that you can control the amount of salt in the final product. The salted peanuts you find in the grocery store are often called "cocktail peanuts" and are meant to be served at bars, where the proprietors prefer very salty snacks to create very thirsty customers!

Smooth Operator™ Peanut Butter

To make 1 cup of smooth natural peanut butter, start with 2 cups of unsalted dry-roasted peanuts, 1 teaspoon of peanut oil, and a pinch of finely ground sea salt. Place the peanuts in a food processor and pulse until the peanuts form a paste. Add half of the oil and continue pulsing for another minute. Continue to add oil and pulse the food processor until the peanut butter is smooth enough for your personal taste. Transfer the peanut butter to a small bowl, add half of the salt, and stir the peanut butter well. Take a taste and add more salt if necessary. Store the peanut butter in a covered glass or plastic container in a cool, dry place.

It is normal for the peanut's natural oil to separate from the peanut butter. If this happens, just stir it back in! Keeping the peanut butter in the refrigerator will help prevent the oil from separating, but it may make it hard to spread.

Crunch Time™ Peanut Butter

Most people think that crunchy peanut butter is prepared like smooth peanut butter, just not ground as fine. This is not so. Crunchy peanut butter is smooth peanut butter with chopped peanuts mixed in. To make crunchy peanut butter, follow the recipe above, but grind just 1 3/4 cups of peanuts. Chop the reserved 1/2 cup and mix it in after you've ground the peanut butter.

Making Flavored Peanut Butters

You can replicate our flavored peanut butters at home as well. Because of the limitations of a home kitchen, these recipes won't taste exactly like our products, but they are close enough to get great-tasting results with all of the recipes in the book.

CINNAMON RAISIN SWIRL™
To 1 cup of smooth natural peanut butter, add 1 tablespoon sugar, 1 teaspoon cinnamon, and 1/4 cup raisins.

THE HEAT IS ON™
To 1 cup of smooth natural peanut butter, add 1 teaspoon crushed red pepper and 1 teaspoon cayenne or hot sauce.

WHITE CHOCOLATE WONDERFUL™
To 1 cup of smooth natural peanut butter, add 2 tablespoons white chocolate chips, gently melted.

DARK CHOCOLATE DREAMS™
To 1 cup of smooth natural peanut butter, add 2 tablespoons semisweet chocolate chips, gently melted.

Peanut Butter Timeline

1818–1845
The first commercial peanut crops are grown in Virginia and North Carolina.

1895
Dr. John Harvey Kellogg patents a "Process of Preparing Nut Meal."

1896
Joseph Lambert, an employee of Dr. Kellogg, begins selling hand-operated peanut butter grinders.

1500 B.C.E.
The Incas of Peru use peanuts as sacrificial offerings and entomb them with their mummies to aid in the spirit life.

1899
Almeeta Lambert, Joseph Lambert's wife, publishes the first peanut butter cookbook, *The Complete Guide to Nut Cookery*.

1890
An unknown doctor experiments by crushing steamed peanuts to create a paste that could be used as an easily digestible protein substitute for patients with no teeth.

1400s
Spanish traders who discover peanuts growing in South America bring peanuts to Africa and China, where they are grown and ground into soups and stews.

1860
Civil War soldiers are reported to dine on "peanut porridge."

1880s
George Washington Carver, considered by many to be the father of the peanut industry, begins his work researching peanuts. Over the course of the next forty years, Carver discovers more than three hundred uses for peanuts, improves peanut horticulture, and popularizes its use as a rotation crop in the South.

1903

George A. Bayle Jr. mechanizes the peanut butter grinding process. A patent for the first automated peanut butter grinder is awarded to Ambrose W. Straub.

1968

The J. M. Smucker Company introduces peanut butter with stripes of jam and jelly in the same jar.

1904

C. H. Sumner introduces peanut butter to the world at the Universal Exposition in St. Louis. Sumner sells $705.11 worth of peanut butter at his concession stand.

1950s

GIs returning from WWII popularize the sandwiches they created out of crackers and rations of peanut butter and jelly.

1958

Jif peanut butter is introduced.

1922

J. L. Rosenfield improves the peanut butter manufacturing process and discovers that adding hydrogenated oil to peanut butter will keep the oil from separating.

1998

Lee Zalben opens the Peanut Butter & Co. sandwich shop in New York City's Greenwich Village, serving classic and newfangled peanut butter sandwiches and featuring new, all-natural flavors.

1928

Rosenfield licenses his patents to the E. K. Pond company, which introduces Peter Pan peanut butter.

1932

Rosenfield introduces his own brand of peanut butter, called Skippy.

chapter 1

breakfast treats

Peanut Butter–Blueberry Muffins

2 cups flour

1 tablespoon baking powder

1 teaspoon salt

¹/₂ cup (1 stick) **unsalted butter,** softened

¹/₂ cup **White Chocolate Wonderful peanut butter** (see p. 13)

1 ¹/₄ cups sugar

1 large egg

1 cup whole milk

1 cup **blueberries,** fresh or frozen (thawed)

There's nothing quite like fresh muffins in the morning; they always have a way of brightening up even the dreariest of days. This is great "wake-up" food—serve them with hot or iced coffee.

MAKES 12 MUFFINS

1. Preheat the oven to 425°F. Grease 12 muffin cups or line with paper liners.

2. In a large bowl, sift together the flour, baking powder, and salt.

3. In another large bowl, using an electric mixer, cream together the butter, peanut butter, and 1 cup of the sugar. Add the egg and milk and mix well. Fold in the flour mixture, and once the dry ingredients are combined, carefully fold in the blueberries. Do not overmix the batter—a few lumps will create a better texture.

4. Pour the batter into the muffin cups and sprinkle the tops with the remaining ¹/₄ cup sugar. Bake for 18 to 20 minutes, or until the tops have risen and are golden brown. Allow to cool before removing from the muffin tins.

Did You Know?

When making a PB&J sandwich, 96 percent of people put the peanut butter on before the jelly.

Orange–Peanut Butter Scones

2 1/2 cups **flour**

1/2 **cup plus 2 tablespoons sugar**

2 teaspoons **baking powder**

1/4 teaspoon **salt**

1/2 **cup** (1 stick) **unsalted butter,** chilled

2 tablespoons **whole milk**

2 tablespoons **orange juice**

2 large **eggs**

1 cup **White Chocolate Wonderful peanut butter** (see p. 13)

2 tablespoons **orange marmalade**

1 tablespoon **freshly grated orange zest**

1 **egg yolk**

2 tablespoons **light or heavy cream**

Tea parties aren't just for little girls anymore! Man or woman, young or old, these tasty scones will inspire you to ring up your pals and invite them over for some good old-fashioned cards and conversation. Any tea will do, but we like these best with a cup of Earl Grey with milk.

MAKES 12 SCONES

1. Preheat the oven to 375°F.

2. In a large bowl, sift together the flour, 1/2 cup sugar, baking powder, and salt. With a pastry blender or two knives, cut the butter into the flour mixture until it resembles coarse meal.

3. In a separate bowl, using an electric mixer, combine the milk, orange juice, eggs, peanut butter, orange marmalade, and orange zest. Pour the wet ingredients into the dry and knead until combined. Try to handle the dough as little as possible, as this will create a more tender scone.

4. Pat the dough into a large round and cut into triangles or use a biscuit cutter to cut into rounds. Place the scones on an ungreased cookie sheet.

5. In a small bowl, whisk together the egg yolk and cream. Brush the mixture on top of each scone to glaze. Sprinkle the remaining 2 tablespoons of sugar over the scones.

6. Bake for 15 to 20 minutes, or until the tops are lightly browned and an inserted toothpick comes out clean. Allow to cool before serving.

NEAT-O!

It takes about 747 peanuts to make one 16-ounce jar of peanut butter.

Peanut Butter & Jelly French Toast

1 can (12 ounces) **frozen grape juice concentrate**

¹/₂ cup Smooth Operator peanut butter

8 slices challah or brioche

4 large eggs

¹/₄ cup whole milk

2 tablespoons unsalted butter

This playful twist on the classic PB&J takes the jelly out of the sandwich and turns it into a fruity syrup—perfect for drizzling or dipping. This dish is great to serve at a big family breakfast or brunch.

MAKES 4 SERVINGS

1. Pour the grape juice concentrate into a small saucepan and simmer uncovered for 20 minutes. Stir constantly, being careful not to let the juice burn.

2. Spread about 2 tablespoons of the peanut butter on 4 slices of bread. Place the other 4 slices of bread atop those covered with peanut butter, pressing down on them lightly, and set aside.

3. In a shallow bowl, whisk together the eggs and milk. Dip both sides of each sandwich in the egg and milk mixture so that the bread is coated evenly.

4. Melt the butter in a large frying pan or skillet over medium heat. Place the sandwiches in the pan. Cook for about 2 minutes per side, or until golden brown.

5. Cut each sandwich in half diagonally and serve with the grape syrup.

Nutty Moments in History

Tom Miller pushed a peanut with his nose to the top of Pikes Peak (altitude 14,110 feet) in 4 days, 23 hours, 47 minutes, and 3 seconds.

Peanut Butter–Banana Pancakes with Honey Butter

Everybody loves pancakes in the morning, and these hearty flapjacks are sure to please even the pickiest of palates. Just don't forget the honey butter—it really makes this recipe sing.

MAKES ABOUT 12 PANCAKES

FOR THE HONEY BUTTER

2 tablespoons honey

1/4 **cup** (1/2 stick) **salted butter,** softened

FOR THE PANCAKES

1 1/4 **cups flour**

2 teaspoons baking powder

1/2 **teaspoon salt**

1 1/2 **cups whole milk**

1 large egg

1 tablespoon sugar

1/4 **cup Smooth Operator peanut butter**

1 ripe banana, chopped

2 to 3 tablespoons unsalted butter

1. To make the honey butter, combine the honey and butter in a small bowl and mix until well incorporated. Refrigerate until ready to serve.

2. To make the pancakes, in a large bowl, sift together the flour, baking powder, and salt.

3. In a blender, combine the milk, egg, sugar, peanut butter, and banana. Pulse until smooth. Add the mixture to the dry ingredients and use a fork to mix just until the dry ingredients are well moistened. The batter may be lumpy.

4. Heat a large griddle over medium heat until a bead of water evaporates on contact. Add 1 to 2 teaspoons of butter, and when it is melted, ladle the batter onto the griddle, using about 1/4 cup batter for each pancake. Cook until golden brown on both sides, about 2 to 3 minutes per side. Continue to add 1 to 2 teaspoons of butter each time you add batter to the griddle. Remove any stray burnt bits of batter by carefully wiping out the griddle with a paper towel between pancakes. Keep the pancakes warm until serving by placing them on an oven-safe serving dish that's been sitting in the oven at 200°F. Serve with the honey butter.

Peanut Butter Waffles

2 cups flour

2 tablespoons baking powder

1/4 teaspoon salt

2 large eggs

1 3/4 cups whole milk

1/4 cup (1/2 stick) **unsalted butter,** melted

1/2 cup sugar

2/3 cup **Cinnamon Raisin Swirl peanut butter** (see p. 13)

Maple syrup, for serving

Waffles, with their rectangular reservoirs for sweet maple syrup, are one of those foods where the fun is "baked right in." The Cinnamon Raisin Swirl peanut butter in this recipe makes these waffles an extra tasty way to start the day, but they're just as good sitting under a scoop of vanilla ice cream.

MAKES 8 WAFFLES

1. Preheat a waffle iron according to the manufacturer's instructions.

2. In a large bowl, sift together the flour, baking powder, and salt.

3. In another large bowl, whisk together the eggs, milk, melted butter, sugar, and peanut butter. Pour the wet ingredients into the dry ingredients and stir until just combined.

4. Grease the hot waffle iron with a small amount of butter. Spoon 1/2 cup (or the amount recommended by the waffle iron's manufacturer) of batter into the center of each section of the waffle iron and close the lid immediately. Bake for about 6 minutes, until the waffle is crisp and golden brown on the outside. Each waffle iron is different, so use the manufacturer's instructions to determine the exact baking time. Serve immediately with maple syrup.

DID YOU KNOW?

There are four types of peanuts grown in the United States: Runner, Virginia, Spanish, and Valencia.

The Peanut Butter & Co. Smoothie

1 cup plain soy milk

3 to 5 large ice cubes

2 tablespoons Smooth Operator peanut butter

1 tablespoon honey

1 large ripe banana

In this go-go-go world, it can be hard to find the time to sit down and have a balanced meal. This smoothie is the perfect solution for those hunger pangs that hit in the morning when you're rushing out the door, and it's a great way to refuel after a workout.

MAKES 1 LARGE SMOOTHIE

1. Pour the soy milk into a blender. Add the ice, peanut butter, honey, and banana.

2. Blend on high speed for 1 to 2 minutes, or until well blended. Drink with a straw in a frosted glass.

Peanut Butter Granola

3 cups rolled oats (not instant)

1 cup roasted peanuts

1/4 cup wheat germ

1/2 cup shredded coconut

1/2 teaspoon ground cinnamon

1/2 teaspoon salt

1 cup canola oil

1 cup honey

1/2 cup Smooth Operator peanut butter

1 teaspoon vanilla extract

1/2 cup raisins

Granola is a delicious and healthful way to energize your day, and as you can see from this recipe, it takes less than an hour to make enough to last at least a week or more. Enjoy with milk, yogurt, or on its own. It's even a tasty topping for ice cream!

MAKES 6 CUPS OF GRANOLA

1. Preheat the oven to 300°F. Grease a 13 x 9-inch baking dish with unsalted butter or light vegetable oil.

2. In a large bowl, combine the oats, peanuts, wheat germ, coconut, cinnamon, and salt.

3. In a small saucepan over low heat, combine the canola oil, honey, peanut butter, and vanilla. Stir until the mixture is completely combined—do not allow to simmer. Pour the warm peanut butter mixture into the bowl with the dry ingredients and mix until well incorporated.

4. Spread the granola in the prepared pan and bake for 30 minutes, or until golden brown. Allow the granola to cool, then break it into chunks. Transfer to an airtight container suitable for storage, add the raisins, and mix until well combined.

chapter 2
sandwiches

The Lunch Box Special™ (PB&J)

2 tablespoons Smooth Operator or Crunch Time peanut butter

2 slices white bread

2 tablespoons grape jelly or strawberry jam

Whether you like yours made with smooth or crunchy peanut butter, with grape jelly or strawberry jam, on white bread or wheat, crusts on or crusts off, chances are peanut butter and jelly was a favorite when you were a kid.

MAKES 1 SANDWICH

1. Spread the peanut butter on one slice of bread, leaving about a 1/2-inch border of bread to account for the "squish factor" when you close the sandwich. Spread the jelly or jam on the other slice of bread in the same fashion.

2. Place the two slices together, and slice in half diagonally.

Note: Never spread the jelly directly on top of the peanut butter, or vice versa. Always clean your knife or spoon of peanut butter before submerging it into the jelly jar. If you break either of these rules, you risk angering others in your household, and neither the author nor the publisher will be held responsible for the consequences.

Lunchbox Lore

How did peanut butter and jelly—that combination of rich, savory peanut butter and sweet jelly—come to be? No one really knows for sure, but when meat was rationed during World War II, vegetarian sources of protein like peanut butter became more popular. Peanut butter was listed on U.S. Army ration menus, and it's believed that savvy soldiers who were still getting used to the taste of peanut butter added jelly to their sandwiches to sweeten them up. The new taste was a hit, and after the war returning GIs popularized the sandwich at home. Wives and mothers found the combination of peanut butter and jelly to be a nutritious, economical, and easy-to-prepare lunch for both their husbands and their children, who began bringing peanut butter and jelly sandwiches to school in droves. To this day, peanut butter and jelly is the most popular sandwich in the lunchroom.

Peanut Butter Club™ (Double-Decker PB&J)

3 slices white bread

4 tablespoons Smooth Operator or Crunch Time peanut butter

2 tablespoons grape jelly or strawberry jam

When we were young, my kid brother loved peanut butter and jelly sandwiches. One day after baseball practice, he joked that he was so hungry he could eat a hundred of them. We didn't have enough bread in the house for that, but I made him this double-decker PB&J, which satisfied his hunger until dinner.

MAKES 1 SANDWICH

1. Toast the bread and immediately spread 2 tablespoons of the peanut butter on one slice of bread. Spread 1 tablespoon of jelly on the second slice of bread and close the sandwich.

2. Gently spread the remaining peanut butter on the top of the sandwich—hold the edges of the top slice to keep it steady. Spread the remaining jelly on the last slice of bread and set it atop the sandwich, jelly side down.

3. Insert two toothpicks, each about 2 inches from opposite corners of the double-decker sandwich, and slice in half diagonally.

Cookie Dough Surprise™

2 tablespoons Smooth Operator or Crunch Time peanut butter

2 slices white bread

2 tablespoons Vanilla Cream Cheese (see p. 35)

2 tablespoons semisweet chocolate chips

When you own a sandwich shop or a restaurant with a small kitchen, you have to find multiple uses for ingredients. I was experimenting with other ways to use our Vanilla Cream Cheese, which is used in the Cinnamon Raisin Swirl Sandwich (see p. 35), and thought to try it with peanut butter and chocolate chips. Much to my surprise, the sandwich reminded me of cookie dough, and a new sandwich was born.

MAKES 1 SANDWICH

1. Spread the peanut butter on one slice of bread and the cream cheese on the other.

2. Sprinkle the chocolate chips on the peanut butter and top with the other slice of bread, cream cheese side down. Slice in half diagonally.

S'more Sandwich™

2 tablespoons Smooth
Operator or Crunch Time
peanut butter

2 slices white bread

12 mini marshmallows

1/2 of a 3/4 ounce milk
chocolate bar

The Girl Scouts invented S'mores, a delicious campfire treat, and we've turned it into a sandwich. Just be careful when eating it right out of the oven: Aside from the fact that the peanut butter, marshmallows, and chocolate inside will be gooey and hot, the combination is deliciously addictive— can you stop at just one?

MAKES 1 SANDWICH

1. Preheat a toaster oven to 300°F.

2. Spread the peanut butter on one side of each slice of bread.

3. Layer the marshmallows and chocolate bar on one slice of bread. Top with the other slice of bread, peanut butter side down.

4. Heat the sandwich in the toaster oven for 2 to 3 minutes, or until the bread is just starting to brown. Remove from the toaster oven and slice in half diagonally.

PB Cup Sandwich™

2 tablespoons Crunch
Time peanut butter

2 slices white bread

2 tablespoons Nutella®

I first encountered Nutella when traveling in Europe. It's an Italian spread made with hazelnuts, cocoa, and skim milk and is a staple all over Europe, where they eat it like, well, peanut butter! This is a rich and decadent sandwich that many people tell me they eat for dessert, not lunch. The crunchy peanut butter really gives this sandwich terrific texture.

MAKES 1 SANDWICH

1. Spread the peanut butter on one slice of bread and the Nutella on the other.

2. Place the two slices together and slice in half diagonally.

The Fluffernutter®

2 tablespoons Smooth
Operator or Crunch Time
peanut butter

2 slices white bread

2 tablespoons
Marshmallow Fluff®

Fluffernutters have been a sweet part of American childhood since 1923, when the then-untitled recipe for the sandwich first appeared on the back of a jar of Marshmallow Fluff.

MAKES 1 SANDWICH

1. Spread the peanut butter on one slice of bread and the Marshmallow Fluff on the other.

2. Place the two slices together and slice in half diagonally.

MARSHMALLOW FLUFF 101

Marshmallow Fluff is the name of the marshmallow cream made by the Durkee Mower Company.

A **Fluffernutter** is the name of the sandwich made with peanut butter and Marshmallow Fluff.

The **Flufferettes** were singers who performed the Fluffernutter jingle on radio shows sponsored by Durkee Mower from the 1930s to the 1950s.

A **Fluffernut** is someone who really likes Marshmallow Fluff.

THIS VINTAGE SUPERMARKET SIGN ADVERTISES
MARSHMALLOW FLUFF IN ITS CLASSIC PEANUT BUTTER UNION.

Dark Chocolate Dreams Sandwich™

2 tablespoons Dark
Chocolate Dreams peanut
butter (see p. 13)

2 slices white bread

2 tablespoons cherry
preserves

1 tablespoon shredded
coconut

When I was a little kid, my grandparents would sometimes take me out for lunch to a local diner, where there was a huge glass case filled with the fanciest-looking cakes I'd ever seen. The Black Forest cake, with its mounds of whipped cream, cherries, and long curls of chocolate, was my dessert of choice. When I was working on the Peanut Butter & Co. menu, I had an idea to try to model a sandwich after that dessert. I made a sandwich with Dark Chocolate Dreams and cherry preserves, but it needed something more—coconut!

MAKES 1 SANDWICH

1. Spread the peanut butter on one slice of bread and the cherry preserves on the other.

2. Sprinkle the coconut on the peanut butter and top with the other slice of bread, preserves side down. Slice in half diagonally.

White Chocolate Wonderful Sandwich™

2 tablespoons White
Chocolate Wonderful
peanut butter (see p. 13)

2 slices white bread

2 tablespoons orange
marmalade

1 tablespoon sliced
almonds, toasted

For kids everywhere, the highlight of any summer day is the afternoon visit from the ice cream man. Two of my favorites were the Toasted Almond Bar and the Orange Creamsicle. Think of this sandwich as a cross between the two. If you want to get fancy, you can cut the crusts off the bread to create a sandwich fancy enough for tea with the Queen.

MAKES 1 SANDWICH

1. Spread the peanut butter on one slice of bread and the marmalade on the other.

2. Sprinkle the almonds on the peanut butter and top with the other slice of bread, marmalade side down. Slice in half diagonally.

Cinnamon Raisin Swirl Sandwich™

2 tablespoons Cinnamon Raisin Swirl peanut butter (see p. 13)

2 slices whole wheat bread

2 tablespoons Vanilla Cream Cheese (recipe follows)

¼ Granny Smith apple, peeled and thinly sliced

The Cinnamon Raisin Swirl Sandwich is my favorite sandwich at Peanut Butter & Co. With its great combination of flavors and textures, it's like a symphony for your mouth!

MAKES 1 SANDWICH

1. Spread the peanut butter on one slice of bread and the cream cheese on the other.

2. Lay the apple slices on the peanut butter and top with the other slice of bread, cream cheese side down. Slice in half diagonally.

Vanilla Cream Cheese

1 package (8 ounces) **cream cheese,** softened

3 tablespoons confectioners' sugar

1 teaspoon vanilla extract

MAKES ABOUT 1 CUP

Place the cream cheese, confectioners' sugar, and vanilla in a large bowl and use an electric mixer to blend until well combined and slightly fluffy. Do not overwhip. Refrigerate in a sealed container for up to 2 weeks.

The Heat Is On Sandwich™

2 tablespoons The Heat Is On peanut butter (see p. 13)

2 slices white bread

2 tablespoons pineapple preserves

6 ounces (1 small cutlet) **grilled chicken breast,** cut into ½-inch strips

Think of this sandwich as a Thai satay between two pieces of bread. For a vegetarian twist, try it with grilled tofu instead of chicken, or try using mango chutney instead of pineapple preserves. Both versions are also great heated on a grill or in a sandwich press.

MAKES 1 SANDWICH

1. Spread the peanut butter on one slice of bread and the pineapple preserves on the other.

2. Lay the chicken on the peanut butter and top with the other slice of bread, preserves side down. Slice in half diagonally.

The Elvis

This is by far the most popular sandwich at Peanut Butter & Co. It makes a hearty lunch, an economical dinner, and a great late-night snack.

1 tablespoon unsalted butter, softened

2 slices white bread

2 tablespoons Smooth Operator or Crunch Time peanut butter

¹/₂ large ripe banana

4 slices bacon, cooked and crispy (optional)

2 teaspoons honey

MAKES 1 SANDWICH

1. Preheat a grill pan or griddle over medium heat.

2. Spread the butter on one side of each slice of bread. Spread the peanut butter on the other side of each slice of bread.

3. Slice the banana lengthwise to make four thin pieces and place on top of the peanut butter on one slice of bread. Top with the bacon slices (if using) and then drizzle the honey on top of the bacon. Top with the remaining slice of bread, butter side up.

4. Place the sandwich on the grill pan. Cook the sandwich for about 3 minutes on each side, until golden brown and crispy. Remove to a cutting board, slice in half, and serve immediately.

The Legend of The Elvis

The story of The Elvis begins on the evening of February 1, 1976. According to the legend, Elvis was at Graceland entertaining a few friends when someone started talking about an incredible peanut butter sandwich called the Fool's Gold Loaf, served at the Colorado Gold Mine Company near Denver, Colorado. The sandwich was made by hollowing out a loaf of Italian bread and then stuffing it with peanut butter, bananas, bacon, and maybe even jelly. The "loaf" was then either warmed up or deep fried. It reportedly cost $49.95, which even by today's standards (remember, this was the seventies) is quite expensive. Well, the description of that sandwich got everyone's mouth watering, and in no time Elvis had his private jet gassed up and he and his friends were off, in the middle of the night, flying from Memphis to Denver for some peanut butter sandwiches.

It is said that the owner of the restaurant brought the sandwiches to the airport, and Elvis and his friends feasted for more than two hours before flying home. The story also goes that Elvis bought the recipe from the restaurant owner and gave it to Pauline Nicholson, his personal cook, with instructions to always be at the ready if his order came through.

The Pregnant Lady™

2 tablespoons Smooth
Operator or Crunch Time
peanut butter

2 slices white bread

6 bread-and-butter
pickle slices

I admit this peanut butter and pickle sandwich might seem a little strange, and the first time a woman ordered it, we couldn't quite believe it ourselves. She was pregnant and two weeks past due, and said she had this craving. . . . We were relieved to hear that she gave birth to a healthy baby boy the following day. Was it the sandwich that finally did it? No one knows for sure, but this combination has become a favorite. Try serving it with a fizzy drink, such as ginger ale or your favorite lemon-lime soda.

MAKES 1 SANDWICH

1. Spread the peanut butter on one side of each slice of bread.

2. Lay the pickles on the peanut butter on one slice of bread and top with the other slice, peanut butter side down. Slice in half diagonally.

Grilled Cheese with Peanut Butter Sandwich

1 tablespoon unsalted
butter, softened

2 slices white bread

2 tablespoons Smooth
Operator or Crunch Time
peanut butter

3 slices American
cheese, preferably orange
or yellow

The idea of a grilled cheese and peanut butter sandwich may not seem very appealing—at first. But go to almost any vending machine in America and you'll find little packets of orange, cheese-flavored sandwich crackers filled with peanut butter, and who doesn't love those?

MAKES 1 SANDWICH

1. Preheat a grill pan or griddle over medium heat.

2. Spread the butter on one side of each slice of bread. Spread the peanut butter on the other side of one of the slices. Lay the cheese on the peanut butter and top with the other slice of bread, butter side up.

3. Place the sandwich on the grill pan. Cook the sandwich for about 2 minutes on each side, or until golden brown. Remove to a cutting board, slice in half, and serve immediately.

Peanut Butter BLT™

2 slices white bread

2 tablespoons Smooth Operator or Crunch Time peanut butter

4 strips bacon, cooked

2 to 3 pieces green leaf lettuce, washed and trimmed

2 to 3 slices ripe tomato

PEANUT BUTTER FROM THE PAST

SCHOOL BOY PEANUT BUTTER WAS MANUFACTURED BY THE ROGERS COMPANY IN WASHINGTON STATE IN THE 1930s.

When I was researching sandwiches for the Peanut Butter & Co. menu, I came across a number of recipes from the 1950s that combined peanut butter and chopped bacon to make a savory sandwich spread. The idea of combining peanut butter and bacon was intriguing, but after testing it out on some friends, I realized that I needed to jazz the sandwich up a bit. I used whole slices of bacon, added lettuce and tomato, and decided to toast the bread. My new creation got rave reviews from my friends, but in retrospect, I realize that I had basically re-created a BLT sandwich, and just substituted peanut butter for the mayo. Sometimes you have to go backward to go forward! This sandwich is great with a glass of iced tea or cool lemonade.

MAKES 1 SANDWICH

1. Toast the bread and immediately spread the peanut butter on one side of each slice.

2. Layer the bacon, lettuce, and tomato atop the peanut butter on one slice of bread, and then top with the other slice, peanut butter side down.

3. Insert two toothpicks, each about 2 inches from opposite corners of the sandwich, and slice in half diagonally.

chapter 3
"after-school" snacks

Ants on a Log

4 stalks celery

¹/₄ cup Smooth Operator or Crunch Time peanut butter

¹/₂ cup raisins

This no-bake recipe is a well-known kindergarten treat— peanut butter–filled celery sticks make up the logs, and raisins represent the ants marching in a line. This healthful snack is great for kids and kids at heart, and the preparation can be the perfect activity to occupy busy little hands after school.

MAKES 1 TO 2 SERVINGS

1. Wash and clean the celery. Trim it into 4-inch-long pieces.

2. Using a butter knife, fill the celery with peanut butter, wiping any excess off the sides.

3. Arrange the filled celery pieces on a serving plate and place a line of individual raisins on the peanut butter.

Frozen Dark Chocolate–Banana Bites

1 large ripe banana

1 to 2 tablespoons Dark Chocolate Dreams peanut butter (see p. 13)

While we've come up with lots of fun and tasty ways for our customers to enjoy our peanut butter, this recipe was suggested to us by a "health nut" in California who enjoys this cold and creamy treat whenever she's in the mood for a pint of ice cream but wants to eat something more healthful.

MAKES 1 SERVING

1. Slice the banana lengthwise and spread the peanut butter on the cut side of one of the halves.

2. Lay the other banana slice on top of the first, flat side down, as if making a sandwich.

3. Cut the re-formed banana into 1- or 2-inch pieces and wrap each individually in plastic wrap.

4. Freeze for at least 2 hours, or until firm. Allow to thaw for about a minute before eating. Store in the freezer for up to 1 week.

No-Bake Peanut Butter–Oatmeal Cookies

1 ¹/₂ cups rolled oats

1 cup nonfat powdered milk

1 ¹/₂ cups Cinnamon Raisin Swirl peanut butter (see p. 13)

³/₄ cup (1 ¹/₂ sticks) unsalted butter

¹/₄ cup honey

1 teaspoon vanilla extract

These no-bake cookies taste like traditional oatmeal-raisin cookies, but with an added burst of peanut butter in every bite.

MAKES 2 DOZEN COOKIES

1. Preheat the oven or toaster oven to 350°F. Line a cookie sheet with parchment paper.

2. Toast the oats in the oven or toaster oven for 10 minutes, giving them a shake halfway through so they don't burn. Place the toasted oats in a large mixing bowl and combine with the powdered milk.

3. In a medium saucepan over low heat, combine the peanut butter, butter, honey, and vanilla. Cook for 5 minutes, stirring constantly. Pour the hot peanut butter mixture over the rolled oats and stir until the oats are completely coated.

4. Drop tablespoonfuls of the dough onto the prepared cookie sheet. Use a spoon to straighten each cookie into a neat circle. Refrigerate the cookies for at least 1 hour, then allow to set at room temperature for another hour before serving.

Peanut Butter Crispy Rice Treats

3 tablespoons unsalted butter

1 bag (10 ounces, or about 40) marshmallows, or 4 cups miniature marshmallows

³/₄ cup Smooth Operator peanut butter

6 cups crispy rice cereal

You'll find the peanut butter makes these famous marshmallow and crispy rice squares even more delicious.

MAKES 9 LARGE SQUARES

1. Lightly grease an 8-inch square baking dish and set aside.

2. Melt the butter in a large saucepan over low heat. Add the marshmallows and stir until completely melted. Quickly add the peanut butter and stir until well incorporated. Remove from the heat. Transfer to a large bowl, add the cereal, and stir until well coated.

3. Press the mixture evenly into the prepared baking dish. Allow to cool for at least 1 hour. Cut into squares and serve immediately, or store in an airtight container for up to 3 days.

Peanut Butter Popcorn Balls

3/4 cup **Smooth Operator peanut butter**

3/4 **cup light brown sugar**

3/4 **cup light corn syrup**

1/4 **teaspoon salt**

10 cups **popped popcorn** (about 1/2 cup unpopped kernels)

3/4 **cup roasted, salted peanuts,** coarsely chopped

Vegetable oil

Popcorn balls are easy to make and so much fun to eat. Legend has it that the first popcorn balls were made by Mother Nature herself when a strange weather phenomenon hit a farm in Nebraska. On one side of the farm, it was so hot that the corn popped right off the stalk. On the other side of the farm, it rained so hard that the sugar ran off the cane and flowed into the cornfield, where it mixed with the popped corn and voilà . . . the first popcorn balls were born!

MAKES 12 TO 14 POPCORN BALLS

1. Combine the peanut butter, brown sugar, corn syrup, and salt in a saucepan over low heat and whisk together until well combined and heated through.

2. Place the popcorn and peanuts in a very large bowl and drizzle with the warm peanut butter mixture. Stir the mixture to ensure that every piece is evenly coated, and allow to cool for 2 minutes. Apply a light coating of vegetable oil to your hands and shape the mixture into 2- to 3-inch balls.

3. Set the popcorn balls on waxed paper and allow to set for 2 to 3 hours. Store in an airtight container for up to 1 week.

Nutty Moments in History

Peanut butter was the secret behind Mr. Ed, TV's talking horse. The horse's handler put peanut butter on Mr. Ed's teeth, and the horse then moved his lips to rub it off.

Peanut Butter Caramel Apples

6 large Granny Smith apples

2 cups roasted, salted peanuts, chopped

50 individually wrapped caramels (about 1 bag)

¹/₂ cup Smooth Operator peanut butter

¹/₄ cup sweetened condensed milk

Who doesn't love a good old-fashioned caramel apple? In this recipe, the sweet, smooth caramel is complemented by our rich, nutty peanut butter to create a new twist on an old favorite. If you wrap each finished apple in plastic wrap, you can keep these carnival-style treats for up to 2 weeks in the refrigerator. Before you begin, you'll need 6 candy apple sticks (6-inch wooden dowels with a pointed end). Wooden chopsticks cut in half will also work in a pinch.

MAKES 6 APPLES

1. Wash the apples well and allow them to dry completely. Be sure to remove any stickers on the apples. Gently twist the stems until they break off. Firmly insert an apple stick into the center of the bottom of each apple, until the stick is at least three-fourths of the way into the apple.

2. Line a small cookie sheet or platter with waxed paper. Place the chopped peanuts in a large bowl and set aside. Unwrap the caramels and place them in a small saucepan. Add the peanut butter, sweetened condensed milk, and 3 tablespoons of water, and heat over low heat until the mixture is combined and just starting to bubble, stirring constantly.

3. Remove the caramel mixture from the heat and use a spoon or small spatula to coat each apple with the mixture. Roll each apple in the bowl of chopped nuts, pressing the nuts into the peanut butter–caramel coating. Be careful—the caramel will be hot! Set the finished apples on the prepared cookie sheet, and refrigerate them for at least 2 hours to let the caramel set before eating.

PEANUT BUTTER FROM THE PAST

FRANK'S JUMBO PEANUT BUTTER WAS A POPULAR BRAND FROM THE 1900s TO THE 1950s.

Baked Apples with Peanut Butter

¹/₂ cup Cinnamon Raisin Swirl peanut butter (see p. 13)

¹/₂ cup (1 stick) plus 4 teaspoons unsalted butter, softened

4 large red apples, cored

4 teaspoons sugar

Vanilla yogurt or ice cream, for serving

Baked apples are a healthful treat and are a great time-saver because they serve double duty—enjoy them hot in the evening for dessert, and eat the leftovers cold in the morning for breakfast!

MAKES 4 SERVINGS

1. Preheat the oven to 300°F.

2. In a small bowl, mix the peanut butter and the ¹/₂ cup butter until well combined. Spoon the peanut butter mixture into the hollow center of the apples, packing it in tightly. Top each apple with 1 teaspoon of butter and 1 teaspoon of sugar.

3. Set the apples in a baking dish with ¹/₄ cup of water and bake for 20 to 25 minutes, or until the apples are fully cooked. While they're baking, baste the apples once or twice with the juice in the bottom of the pan. Allow to cool for 5 minutes before serving with vanilla yogurt or ice cream.

For Health Nuts

Believe it or not, peanut butter is a health food that tastes great, too! Peanut butter:

• is a vegetarian source of protein

• provides essential vitamins and minerals such as vitamin E, niacin, phosphorous, and magnesium

• is cholesterol free and can help improve your HDL/LDL (good cholesterol/bad cholesterol) ratio

• contains fiber—2 tablespoons of peanut butter offers about as much as ¹/₂ cup of broccoli

• is a good source of folic acid, an essential nutrient during pregnancy and in the prevention of heart disease

NUT-LET

Just Doctor Peanuts'
Method
Health ✿ Help ✿ Habit ✿ Recipes

FROM THE VERY BEGINNING, DOCTORS KNEW THAT PEANUT BUTTER WAS A HEALTHFUL FOOD.

Peanut Butter Banana Bread

2 cups flour

1 teaspoon baking powder

1/2 teaspoon baking soda

1 teaspoon salt

1/2 cup vegetable shortening

1 cup sugar

1 cup Smooth Operator peanut butter

1 1/2 cups mashed very ripe bananas

2 large eggs

Vanilla ice cream or Marshmallow Fluff, for serving

Whenever we have too many bananas at home, we wait for them to ripen up and make fresh banana bread. Peanut butter and bananas are a great combination, and this peanut butter–flavored banana bread makes for a very satisfying snack or dessert.

MAKES ABOUT 12 SERVINGS

1. Preheat the oven to 350°F. Butter and flour the bottom and sides of a 9-inch loaf pan. Cut a piece of parchment paper or brown paper bag to fit the bottom of the loaf pan.

2. In a large bowl, sift together the flour, baking powder, baking soda, and salt and set aside.

3. In a separate large bowl, use an electric mixer to cream together the shortening and sugar. Add the peanut butter, bananas, and the eggs, one at a time, and continue mixing until well incorporated. Fold in the flour mixture and pour the batter into the prepared loaf pan.

4. Bake for 60 to 70 minutes, or until the top is golden brown and splits in the middle. Serve warm or at room temperature with a scoop of vanilla ice cream or a dollop of Marshmallow Fluff.

Nutty Moments in History

The world's largest PB&J sandwich was created in Oklahoma City, Oklahoma, on September 7, 2002, by the Oklahoma Peanut Commission and the Oklahoma Wheat Commission. The sandwich weighed in at nearly 900 pounds and contained 350 pounds of peanut butter and 144 pounds of jelly. Now that's one giant sandwich!

OLD-FASHIONED PEANUT BUTTER COOKIES AND CHOCOLATE CHIP–PEANUT BUTTER COOKIES (P. 50)

Old-Fashioned Peanut Butter Cookies

2 1/2 cups flour

1 teaspoon baking powder

1 teaspoon baking soda

1 teaspoon salt

1 1/4 cups Smooth Operator peanut butter

1 cup vegetable shortening

1 teaspoon vanilla extract

1 cup granulated sugar

1 cup light brown sugar, packed

2 large eggs

These Old-Fashioned Peanut Butter Cookies are the very same recipe we serve in our sandwich shop in Greenwich Village. We sell hundreds every week—people tell us they love the light, flaky texture, the rich peanut butter flavor, and the familiar crisscross pattern on top.

MAKES 3 DOZEN COOKIES

1. Preheat the oven to 350°F.

2. In a large bowl, sift together the flour, baking powder, baking soda, and salt and set aside.

3. In a separate large bowl, use an electric mixer to combine the peanut butter, shortening, and vanilla. Add the granulated sugar and brown sugar and mix until fluffy. Add the eggs, one at a time, and continue mixing until well combined. Add the dry ingredients, 1/2 cup at a time, mixing until the dough is firm.

4. Use a tablespoon to make 1-inch balls of dough and set them 3 inches apart on an ungreased cookie sheet. Using a fork, press down on each cookie twice, making a crisscross pattern on the top of the cookie.

5. Bake on the center rack of the oven for 10 to 12 minutes, or until golden. Allow to cool 5 to 10 minutes before serving. Store in an airtight container for up to 2 weeks.

Did You Know?

Peanut butter is consumed in 89 percent of American households.

Chocolate Chip–Peanut Butter Cookies

1 cup flour

3/4 teaspoon baking soda

3/4 cup (1 1/2 sticks) unsalted butter, softened

3/4 cup Smooth Operator peanut butter

1/4 cup granulated sugar

3/4 cup light brown sugar

1 teaspoon vanilla extract

1 large egg

1 cup semisweet chocolate chips

I like my chocolate chip cookies big and crispy, but still a little chewy on the inside. These cookies really are mouth-watering, and you should be warned—they are addictive, so bake with caution.

MAKES 18 COOKIES

1. In a large bowl, sift together the flour and baking soda and set aside.

2. In a separate large bowl, use an electric mixer to cream together the butter, peanut butter, granulated sugar, brown sugar, and vanilla. Add the egg and continue mixing. Add the dry ingredients, 1/2 cup at a time, mixing until the dough is firm. If the dough is too dry, add water by the tablespoon (but no more than a 1/4 cup) until it is moist and easier to work with. Fold in the chocolate chips.

3. Transfer the dough to a cutting board and shape into a log 2 1/2 to 3 inches wide. Wrap the cookie dough in plastic wrap and refrigerate for 1 hour.

4. Preheat the oven to 350°F. Remove the cookie dough from the refrigerator and cut into slices 1/4 to 1/3-inch thick. Place the cookies on a cookie sheet at least 1 inch apart and bake for 10 to 12 minutes. Allow to cool before serving. Store in an airtight container for up to 2 weeks.

NEAT-O!

The amount of peanut butter eaten in a year could wrap the Earth in a ribbon of 16-ounce peanut butter jars one and one-third times.

Peanut Butter Shortbread

2 cups flour

3/4 teaspoon salt

1 cup (2 sticks) unsalted butter, softened

3/4 cup Smooth Operator peanut butter

1 cup sugar

1 teaspoon vanilla

1/4 cup semisweet chocolate chips

Shortbread is a rich, sweet Scottish biscuit traditionally eaten on Christmas and New Year's Day. The secret to great shortbread is the butter, which Scottish dairy farmers had plenty of. Shortbread is traditionally baked in a round pan and served in wedges that resemble the rays of the sun. This peanut butter shortbread follows that tradition and adds chocolate chips for extra indulgence.

MAKES 12 PIECES OF SHORTBREAD

1. Preheat the oven to 275°F. Grease a 9-inch cake pan.

2. In a large bowl, sift together the flour and salt and set aside.

3. In a separate large bowl, use an electric mixer to combine the butter, peanut butter, sugar, and vanilla until fluffy. Continue mixing, adding the dry ingredients 1/2 cup at a time until fully incorporated.

4. Press the dough into the prepared cake pan. Use a knife to score the surface of the dough into 12 wedge-shaped pieces. Repeatedly press the tips of the tines of a fork around the outer edge of the shortbread, creating four concentric circles of dots. Press 3 chocolate chips into each wedge of shortbread.

5. Bake for 75 minutes, or until the shortbread is a pale golden color, not brown. Allow to cool for 1 hour before using a knife to cut out the wedges. Store in an airtight container for up to 2 weeks.

Peanut Butter Biscotti

3 cups flour

2 teaspoons baking powder

1/2 teaspoon salt

1 cup roasted, salted peanuts, coarsely chopped

1 cup semisweet chocolate chips

6 tablespoons unsalted butter, softened

3/4 cup Smooth Operator peanut butter

1 cup plus 2 tablespoons sugar

1 tablespoon vanilla extract

4 large eggs

Biscotti are long, thin Italian cookies that are served with wine or coffee, usually after a meal. Biscotti are fairly crunchy, and in fact, the word biscotti *means "twice-baked" in Italian.*

MAKES 18 COOKIES

1. Preheat the oven to 350°F.

2. Sift together the flour, baking powder, and salt in a large bowl. Add the peanuts and chocolate chips and set aside.

3. In a separate large bowl, use an electric mixer to cream together the butter, peanut butter, 1 cup sugar, and vanilla. Add 3 of the eggs, one at a time, until they are well incorporated. Slowly add the dry ingredients to the wet, continuing to mix until the dough is smooth.

4. Divide the dough into 2 portions, and form each into a log approximately 3 inches in diameter. Place the logs on an ungreased cookie sheet about 3 to 4 inches apart and flatten them slightly with the palm of your hand. Beat the remaining egg and brush onto the top and sides of the logs. Sprinkle with the remaining 2 tablespoons sugar. Bake for 25 to 30 minutes, or until golden brown. Keep an eye on the bottom to make sure the loaves aren't burning. Remove from the oven.

5. Reduce the oven temperature to 300°F. Let the logs cool for 10 minutes, then cut them into slices about 3/4 inch thick. Place the slices, cut side down, on the cookie sheet and bake, turning once, until crisp, an additional 7 minutes on each side. These cookies will stay fresh for 3 to 4 months if kept in an airtight container.

Peanut Butter Meringue Cookies

2 egg whites, cold

Pinch of salt

²/₃ cup confectioners' sugar, sifted

¹/₂ cup Smooth Operator peanut butter

1 teaspoon vanilla extract

¹/₄ cup roasted, salted peanuts, chopped

These flourless cookies are light and crunchy. The peanut butter makes a heavier batter than traditional meringues, creating crisp, flat cookies. Fun to eat on their own, they also make a great crunchy topping when crumbled on ice cream or yogurt.

MAKES 2 DOZEN MERINGUES

1. Preheat the oven to 175°F. Cover 2 cookie sheets with parchment paper and set aside.

2. In a very clean metal bowl, combine the egg whites and salt and beat with an electric mixer until stiff peaks form. Continue mixing on low speed, slowly adding the confectioners' sugar. Once the sugar has been incorporated, gently fold in the peanut butter and vanilla.

3. Drop tablespoonfuls of batter onto the prepared cookie sheets. Sprinkle each cookie with chopped peanuts. Bake for 2 hours, or until completely dry to the touch. Allow the cookies to cool completely before removing from the pan.

Nutty Moments in History

Adrian Finch of Australia holds the Guinness World Record for peanut throwing, launching the lovable legume 111 feet, 10 inches in 1999 to claim the record.

PEANUT BUTTER BLONDIES (P. 56) AND PEANUT BUTTER SWIRL BROWNIES

Peanut Butter Swirl Brownies

FOR THE BROWNIES

1/2 cup flour

1/4 teaspoon salt

1/2 cup (1 stick) **unsalted butter**

3 ounces (1/2 cup) **semi-sweet chocolate chips**

1 teaspoon vanilla extract

1 cup light brown sugar

2 large eggs

FOR THE PEANUT BUTTER TOPPING

1/2 cup Smooth Operator peanut butter

1/2 cup (1 stick) **unsalted butter**

1/2 cup brown sugar

1 large egg

1/4 cup flour

No one knows who actually baked the first brownie, but most people chalk it up to a busy cook who forgot to add the baking powder to a chocolate cake batter. My mom used to bake these moist, chewy brownies with a rich peanut butter topping when I went home from college for a visit—they were a welcome treat for my friends and me after many months away from home.

MAKES 12 BROWNIES

1. Preheat the oven to 350°F. Butter the bottom and sides of an 8-inch square baking dish. Dust the pan with flour and tap out the excess.

2. To make the brownie batter, in a large bowl, sift together the flour and salt and set aside.

3. In a medium saucepan over low heat, combine the butter, chocolate chips, and vanilla and stir until smooth. Remove from heat and add the brown sugar, stirring quickly until well incorporated. Set aside and allow to cool for 2 to 3 minutes.

4. Transfer the chocolate mixture to a large bowl and add the eggs, one at a time, stirring constantly to avoid cooking the eggs. Fold in the dry ingredients and pour the batter into the prepared pan.

5. To make the peanut butter topping, in a medium saucepan over low heat, stir the peanut butter, butter, and brown sugar until smooth. Remove from the heat and transfer to a mixing bowl. Allow to cool for 2 to 3 minutes and then add the egg, stirring quickly. Fold in the flour.

6. Pour the peanut butter topping over the brownie batter. Using a butter knife, cut a series of lines horizontally and vertically through the batters to make a criss-cross pattern. Bake for 40 minutes. Allow to cool completely before cutting into squares. Enjoy with a cold glass of milk.

Peanut Butter Blondies

1 1/2 cups flour

1 teaspoon baking powder

1/2 teaspoon baking soda

1/2 teaspoon salt

1/2 cup nonfat sour cream

1 cup Smooth Operator peanut butter

1/2 cup applesauce

1 tablespoon vanilla extract

1 1/2 cups light brown sugar

1 large egg

Most people think of blondies as vanilla versions of the ever-popular chocolate brownie. These peanut butter blondies are lighter in color than chocolate brownies, and lower in fat and calories, too. But if you don't tell anyone, we won't either. Serve with a glass of cold milk.

MAKES 12 BLONDIES

1. Preheat the oven to 350°F. Butter the bottom and sides of an 11 x 7-inch baking pan. Dust the pan with flour and tap out the excess.

2. In a large bowl, sift together the flour, baking powder, baking soda, and salt and set aside.

3. In a separate large bowl, use an electric mixer to beat together the sour cream, peanut butter, applesauce, and vanilla. Add the brown sugar and then the egg and mix until well incorporated. Fold in the dry ingredients and, when well combined, pour into the baking dish.

4. Bake for 15 to 20 minutes, or until an inserted toothpick comes out clean. Do not overbake. Allow to cool completely before cutting into bars.

Did You Know?

Peanuts are not a nut! Botanically classified as legumes, peanuts contain properties of both the bean/lentil and tree nut families.

Peanut Butter Cupcakes with Chocolate Fudge Frosting

1 1/4 cups flour

1 1/2 teaspoons baking powder

1/2 teaspoon salt

1 cup light brown sugar

6 tablespoons (3/4 stick) unsalted butter, softened

1 teaspoon vanilla extract

1/2 cup Smooth Operator peanut butter

2 large eggs

1/2 cup whole milk

Chocolate Fudge Frosting (recipe follows)

1 1/3 cup heavy cream

1 bag (12 ounces) semisweet chocolate chips

When I was in elementary school, a birthday meant bringing homemade cupcakes to school to give out before recess. Before sending these cupcakes to school, please check to make sure that no one in the class has any nut allergies.

MAKES 1 DOZEN CUPCAKES

1. Preheat the oven to 350°F. Line 12 muffin cups with paper baking cups.

2. In a large bowl, sift together the flour, baking powder, and salt and set aside.

3. In a separate large bowl, cream together the brown sugar, butter, and vanilla with an electric mixer. Add the peanut butter and beat until smooth. Add the eggs one at a time, beating well after each addition, and then add the milk. Slowly add the flour mixture and combine until the batter is uniform. Do not overmix.

4. Fill the prepared muffin cups with the batter until they are almost full. Bake for 20 minutes, or until the cupcakes spring back when touched lightly. Let the cupcakes cool completely before icing with Chocolate Fudge Frosting.

Chocolate Fudge Frosting

MAKES ABOUT 2 CUPS

1. In a medium sized saucepan over medium heat bring the cream to a light simmer. Transfer the hot cream to a bowl and add the chocolate chips. Allow the cream and chocolate to sit undisturbed for five minutes, then stir until smooth. Refrigerate for at least 2 hours, or until the icing is chilled throughout and firm.

2. Use an electric mixer to beat the icing until creamy and spreadable. Be careful not to over-whip. Spread on the cup cakes immediately.

Peanut Butter & Jelly Cupcakes

1½ cups flour

1½ teaspoons baking powder

½ teaspoon salt

½ cup (1 stick) unsalted butter, softened

1 cup sugar

1 teaspoon vanilla extract

2 large eggs

½ cup whole milk

¾ cup strawberry jam or preserves

2 cups Peanut Butter Frosting (see p. 82)

Addicted to PB&J sandwiches? These traditional vanilla cupcakes filled with strawberry jam and topped with creamy Peanut Butter Frosting are a special treat for kids and adults alike, and always sell out at the school bake sale. Before sending these cupcakes to school, please check with your child's teacher to make sure that no one in the class has any nut allergies.

MAKES 1 DOZEN CUPCAKES

1. Preheat the oven to 350°F. Line 12 muffin cups with paper baking cups.

2. In a large bowl, sift together the flour, baking powder, and salt and set aside.

3. In a separate large bowl, cream together the butter, sugar, and vanilla with an electric mixer. Add the eggs, one at a time, beating well after each addition, then add the milk. Slowly add the flour mixture and combine until the batter is uniform. Do not overmix.

4. Fill each cupcake liner halfway with batter. Drop a tablespoon of the jam in the center of each cupcake and then top with more batter so that they are a little more than three-quarters full.

5. Bake for 20 minutes, or until the cupcakes spring back when touched lightly. Let them cool completely before icing with Peanut Butter Frosting.

PEANUT BUTTER & JELLY CUPCAKES AND PEANUT BUTTER CUPCAKES WITH CHOCOLATE FUDGE FROSTING (P. 57)

Peanut Butter & Jelly Milk Shake

3 scoops vanilla ice cream

2 tablespoons Smooth Operator peanut butter

2 tablespoons strawberry preserves

$^1/_2$ cup whole milk

1 tablespoon vanilla syrup

Great with burgers, sandwiches, or all on its own, the milk shake is an integral part of American diner and soda shop culture.

MAKES 1 SERVING

1. Place the ice cream in the blender pitcher. Add the peanut butter and preserves, followed by the milk, and finally the flavored syrup.

2. Blend on a low speed until the ingredients are mixed, then on a higher speed until the mixture reaches a smooth, thick consistency. If the shake is hard to blend, try adding more milk to the blender, or turn off the machine completely and use a long-handled spoon to shift the ingredients.

Shake It Up!

Follow the instructions above to make these great peanut butter milk shakes.

FLUFFERNUTTER SHAKE

3 scoops vanilla ice cream

2 tablespoons Smooth Operator peanut butter

2 tablespoons Marshmallow Fluff

$^1/_2$ cup whole milk

1 tablespoon vanilla syrup

CHOCOLATE–PEANUT BUTTER SHAKE

3 scoops chocolate ice cream

2 tablespoons Smooth Operator peanut butter

$^1/_2$ cup whole milk

1 tablespoon chocolate syrup

PEANUT BUTTER HAS ALWAYS BEEN A FAVORITE AT ICE CREAM PARLORS AND SODA FOUNTAINS.

Peanut Butter Hot Chocolate

2 1/2 cups milk

1 teaspoon vanilla extract

1/2 cup unsweetened cocoa powder

1/2 cup sugar

2 1/2 cups light cream

2/3 cup Dark Chocolate Dreams peanut butter (see p. 13)

Mini marshmallows, whipped cream, or Marshmallow Fluff, for serving

There's nothing like coming home to rich hot chocolate on a cold winter day. This special recipe is sure to warm the body as well as the soul.

MAKES 4 SERVINGS

1. In a medium saucepan, heat the milk and vanilla until hot. Whisk in the cocoa and sugar and continue stirring until dissolved. Add the cream and peanut butter and let simmer for 3 to 5 minutes, stirring constantly.

2. Serve in warm mugs with mini marshmallows, a big dollop of whipped cream, or Marshmallow Fluff.

Peanut Butter Dog Biscuits

Peanut butter isn't just a great snack for people—it's a healthy treat for dogs, too! Try rewarding your favorite pooch's good behavior with one of these tasty treats.

**2 cups whole wheat flour • 1 cup rolled oats • 1/2 cup yellow cornmeal
1 cup Smooth Operator peanut butter • 2 tablespoons honey • 1 large egg
2 tablespoons peanut or canola oil**

MAKES ABOUT 2 DOZEN BISCUITS

1. Preheat the oven to 350°F.

2. In a medium bowl, combine the flour, oats, and cornmeal and set aside.

3. In a large bowl, combine the peanut butter, honey, egg, and peanut oil with 1 cup of water and mix until well incorporated. Slowly add the dry ingredients, stirring until combined.

4. Turn the dough out onto a lightly floured surface and roll to a 1/4-inch thickness. With a bone-shaped cookie cutter, cut out biscuits and transfer to an ungreased cookie sheet. Bake for 30 to 40 minutes, or until golden brown. Cool before serving to your pooch.

chapter 4
savory snacks, entrées & sides

SWEET AND SPICY PEANUT BUTTER–GLAZED CHICKEN TENDERS (P. 64)

Sweet and Spicy Peanut Butter–Glazed Chicken Tenders

1/3 cup **honey**

1/4 cup **The Heat Is On peanut butter** (see p. 13)

1/4 cup (1/2 stick) **unsalted butter**

2 large boneless, skinless chicken breasts, cut into 1- to 2-inch strips

These chicken tenders are a great lunch. Eat them on their own or on a roll as a sandwich with some fresh greens. You can even chop them up and roll the chicken in lettuce leaves for an authentic Asian appetizer. This is also a great way to prepare spicy Buffalo-style chicken wings.

MAKES 4 SERVINGS

1. Preheat the oven to 350°F. Prepare a 9 x 13-inch glass baking dish by lining it with aluminum foil (this will make cleanup a snap).

2. In a small saucepan over low heat, combine the honey, peanut butter, and butter until the butter is melted and the mixture is smooth. Do not let the glaze boil. Remove from the heat.

3. Dip the chicken strips in the glaze, coating well on both sides. Reserve the extra glaze. Place the coated strips in the foil-lined pan, cover with aluminum foil, and cook for 20 minutes on the center rack of the oven.

4. Remove the foil cover and pour the remaining glaze on top of the chicken. Continue to roast for another 20 minutes, or until the chicken is cooked through.

PEANUT BUTTER FROM THE PAST

THE D & L SLADE CO. WAS A SPICE MILL THAT FOUND SUCCESS WHEN THEY ADDED PEANUT BUTTER TO THEIR ROSTER OF PRODUCTS.

Peanut Butter Barbecued Chicken

4 boneless chicken breasts

Peanut Butter Barbecue Sauce (recipe follows)

$^1/_4$ **cup vegetable oil**

1 medium yellow onion, finely chopped

2 cloves garlic, minced

$^1/_2$ **cup tomato paste**

$^1/_2$ **cup honey**

$^1/_4$ **cup The Heat Is On peanut butter** (see p. 13)

3 tablespoons apple cider vinegar

2 tablespoons light brown sugar

3 tablespoons light soy sauce

1 tablespoon black pepper, freshly ground

Slow-cooked barbecue is one of the simple pleasures in life, and believe it or not, peanut butter adds a nutty flavor to barbecue that can't be beat. This sauce is great for preparing chicken, as a topping for burgers, and as a dipping sauce for French fries.

MAKES 4 SERVINGS

1. Slather the chicken with the Peanut Butter Barbecue Sauce.

2. Cook the chicken on a grill for about 15 minutes on each side, or until cooked throughout. If cooking indoors, use a grill pan over high heat.

Peanut Butter Barbecue Sauce

MAKES ABOUT 2 CUPS

Heat the oil in a medium-sized saucepan over medium heat. Add the onion and garlic and sauté until translucent. Reduce the heat to low and add the tomato paste, honey, peanut butter, vinegar, brown sugar, soy sauce, and pepper. Add $^1/_4$ cup water and mix until well combined. Let simmer for 10 minutes, stirring frequently. For a smooth sauce, process in a blender. Allow to cool before using.

Juicy Peanut Butter–Marinated Pork Tenderloin

2 pork tenderloins,
³/₄ pounds each

Peanut Butter Marinade
(recipe follows)

Peanut or olive oil,
for the pan

¹/₄ **cup Smooth Operator**
peanut butter

¹/₄ **cup apricot preserves**

3 tablespoons peanut oil

3 tablespoons apple cider
vinegar

1 medium yellow onion,
peeled and quartered

1 clove garlic

1 tablespoon grated fresh
ginger

¹/₂ **tablespoon black**
pepper, freshly ground

This pork tenderloin recipe is so easy to prepare, and it seems to please even the most picky eaters. The sweet and savory marinade creates a flavorful dish that is sure to become a family favorite. Serve with creamy mashed potatoes and steamed or sautéed broccoli.

MAKES 4 SERVINGS

1. Immerse the pork in the Peanut Butter Marinade and cover. Refrigerate for 4 to 6 hours.

2. Preheat the oven to 375°F. Remove most of the marinade from the meat and reserve.

3. Sear the pork in peanut or olive oil in a hot skillet for about 5 minutes on each side, or until brown.

4. Transfer the tenderloins to a baking dish and pour the reserved marinade over the meat. Cook covered for 8 minutes, then continue cooking uncovered until a meat thermometer inserted in the thickest part of the meat reads 150°F. For best results, allow the meat to rest for 5 minutes, then slice and serve.

Peanut Butter Marinade

MAKES ABOUT 2 CUPS

Combine the peanut butter, apricot preserves, peanut oil, vinegar, onion, garlic, ginger, and pepper in a food processor and pulse until well combined.

Did You Know?

Two peanut farmers have been elected president of the United States: Thomas Jefferson and Jimmy Carter.

Peanut Butter and Maple Glazed Ham

1 fully cooked bone-in ham (about 14 pounds)

Whole cloves, for studding ham

1/2 cup maple syrup

1/2 cup apple jelly

2 tablespoons apple cider vinegar

2/3 cup Smooth Operator peanut butter

This year, serve up a holiday ham like no other. The peanut butter flavor in this glaze is not overpowering and adds just enough nutty nuance to make the dish unforgettable.

MAKES 8 TO 10 SERVINGS

1. Preheat the oven to 350°F.

2. With a knife, lightly score the top of the ham, forming a crisscross pattern. Stud the center of each diamond with a clove. Bake the ham in a roasting pan on the center rack of the oven for 1 hour.

3. In a small saucepan, combine the maple syrup, apple jelly, vinegar, and peanut butter and simmer over low heat for 10 minutes, until syrupy.

4. Baste the ham with the glaze and cook for an additional 30 to 35 minutes, or until the glaze is brown and bubbly. Transfer the ham to a platter and let stand for 15 minutes before carving.

Spicy Peanut Butter Burgers

1 1/2 pounds ground beef or turkey

1/2 cup The Heat Is On peanut butter (see p. 13)

2 tablespoons unsalted butter

1 yellow onion, grated

1 large egg

3 tablespoons bread crumbs

Olive oil, for the pan

How to make a better burger? Add peanut butter, of course! Serve these burgers on fresh buns with lettuce, tomatoes, and your favorite ketchup or barbecue sauce.

MAKES ABOUT 8 BURGERS

1. In a large bowl, combine the ground meat, peanut butter, butter, onion, egg, and bread crumbs and knead with your hands until well combined.

2. Make patties about 4 inches wide and 3/4 inch thick. Refrigerate for 1 to 2 hours to allow the patties to set and the flavors to meld.

3. Grill the burgers on an outdoor grill for best results, or fry in a skillet with a small amount of olive oil for 2 to 3 minutes on each side, or until fully cooked inside.

Thai-Style Shrimp Skewers

1 large red onion,
cut into 1-inch pieces

8 cherry tomatoes,
sliced in half

2 bell peppers,
red and/or green,
cut into 1-inch squares

1 small pineapple,
peeled and cut into 1-inch
cubes (about 2 cups)

16 large shrimp,
raw, peeled and deveined,
with the tails on

Spicy Peanut Sauce
(recipe follows)

Everyone goes nuts for food on a stick! This recipe is sure to be one you'll want to add to your grilling repertoire. For a vegetarian version, just substitute firm tofu for the shrimp. For appetizer portions (pictured), break each skewer in half before serving.

MAKES 4 SERVINGS OR 16 APPETIZER SKEWERS

1. Soak 8 wooden skewers in water for 1 to 2 hours to keep them from burning on the grill.

2. Place the items to be grilled on the skewers in the following order: onion, tomato, pepper, pineapple, shrimp. Repeat so that each skewer has 2 pieces of shrimp.

3. Brush on the Spicy Peanut Sauce and grill over medium heat for 3 to 5 minutes on each side. Use the extra sauce for dipping.

Spicy Peanut Sauce

1 small yellow onion,
chopped

2 cloves garlic

¼ cup chopped fresh cilantro

1 teaspoon grated fresh ginger

1 tablespoon freshly squeezed lime juice

1 can (14 ounces) **coconut milk**

½ cup Smooth Operator peanut butter

¼ cup The Heat Is On peanut butter (see p. 13)

2 tablespoons sesame oil

2 tablespoons rice vinegar

1 tablespoon honey

MAKES ABOUT 2 CUPS

Combine the onion, garlic, cilantro, ginger, lime juice, coconut milk, smooth peanut butter, spicy peanut butter, sesame oil, vinegar, and honey in a food processor and blend until smooth.

Note: You can vary the level of spiciness by changing the ratio of smooth to spicy peanut butter.

Peanut Butter Veggie Burgers

1 large portabella mushroom cap, finely chopped

1 medium yellow onion, finely chopped

1 medium red bell pepper, finely chopped

1 large carrot, peeled and grated

2 cloves garlic, finely chopped

2 large eggs

1/3 cup Smooth Operator peanut butter

1 cup fresh bread crumbs

1/2 teaspoon salt

1 teaspoon black pepper, freshly ground

3 tablespoons olive oil

Some of my vegetarian friends were lamenting one day about the lack of a really good veggie burger recipe. The frozen patties they bought at the supermarket tasted too much like meat, and the powdered mixes were too crumbly to keep their shape in the pan. "Would adding peanut butter help?" they asked me. This is a hearty, tasty veggie burger that uses fresh vegetables to create a new taste sensation for your favorite bun.

MAKES ABOUT 6 BURGERS

1. Mix together the mushroom, onion, bell pepper, carrot, and garlic in a large bowl. Add the eggs, peanut butter, bread crumbs, salt, and pepper and mix until well combined.

2. With wet hands, shape the mixture into 6 patties and refrigerate for 30 minutes.

3. In a large skillet, heat the olive oil over medium heat and fry the patties about 10 minutes on each side. Allow the burgers to rest for 2 to 3 minutes before serving.

Nutty Moments in History

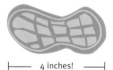

|—— 4 inches! ——|

The world's largest peanut was 4 inches long and was grown by Earl Adkins in North Carolina.

Vegetarian Chili

1/4 cup **olive oil**

2 **medium-sized yellow onions,** chopped

4 **cloves garlic,** minced

1 **package** (14 ounces) **firm tofu**

1/2 **teaspoon salt**

1 **tablespoon black pepper,** freshly ground

2 **teaspoons paprika**

2 **cans** (14.5 ounces each) **diced tomatoes**

1 **can** (12 ounces) **tomato paste**

2 **cups vegetable stock**

2 **cans** (15 ounces each) **kidney beans,** rinsed and drained

1 **can** (15 ounces) **black beans,** rinsed and drained

1 **can** (15 ounces) **white beans,** rinsed and drained

1 **can** (15 ounces) **whole sweet corn,** rinsed and drained

1 cup **The Heat Is On peanut butter** (see p. 13)

Crushed red pepper (optional)

It seems like everyone I know has a secret family recipe for chili. Some are quite exotic, and some take hours to prepare. For this recipe, I tried to create a great-tasting dish that used easy-to-find ingredients and would be ready to eat in less than an hour. You can use ground beef or turkey instead of crumbled tofu for a more traditional version if you like. Serve over rice or mashed potatoes, or for Cincinnati-style chili, serve over spaghetti.

MAKES 8 SERVINGS

1. In a large stockpot, heat the olive oil over medium heat. Add the onions, garlic, tofu, salt, pepper, and paprika and sauté until the onions and garlic are translucent.

2. Add the diced tomatoes and their liquid to the pot and simmer for 5 minutes. Add the tomato paste and vegetable stock and simmer for 10 minutes. Add the kidney beans, black beans, white beans, and corn and simmer for 10 minutes.

3. Reduce the heat to low and stir the peanut butter into the chili. Add additional crushed red pepper to increase the spiciness if desired.

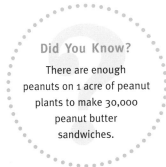

Did You Know?

There are enough peanuts on 1 acre of peanut plants to make 30,000 peanut butter sandwiches.

African Peanut Butter Soup (Mafé)

3 tablespoons
vegetable oil

1 large yellow onion,
finely chopped

2 cloves garlic, minced

6 cups vegetable or
chicken stock

1 cup Smooth Operator
peanut butter

2 large sweet potatoes,
peeled and cut into
1/2-inch cubes

1 can (14.5 ounces)
crushed plum tomatoes

1/2 teaspoon
cayenne pepper

1/2 teaspoon
ground coriander

1/2 teaspoon
ground cumin

1/2 teaspoon salt

1/2 teaspoon black
pepper, freshly ground

Sour cream or plain
yogurt, for garnish

Chopped parsley,
for garnish

Roasted, salted peanuts,
coarsely chopped,
for garnish

This creamy, tomato-based peanut soup is based on traditional African soups that are still served in small villages today. You can add some chicken to make this soup a meal.

MAKES 6 SERVINGS

1. In a large stockpot, heat the vegetable oil over medium heat and sauté the onion and garlic until translucent.

2. Add the stock and peanut butter and stir. Once the peanut butter has been incorporated, stir in the sweet potatoes, crushed tomatoes with their liquid, cayenne pepper, coriander, cumin, salt, and pepper and simmer for 45 minutes.

3. Garnish with your choice of sour cream or yogurt, parsley, and chopped peanuts.

Thai Peanut Soup

2 tablespoons peanut oil (or other light vegetable oil)

1 large yellow onion, finely chopped

2 cloves garlic, minced

6 cups vegetable or chicken stock

1 package (14 ounces) extra-firm tofu, cut into 1/2-inch cubes

1 can (15 ounces) straw mushrooms, rinsed and drained

1/2 cup freshly squeezed lime juice

1/4 cup finely chopped lemongrass

1 tablespoon grated fresh ginger

4 large bay leaves

1/3 cup Smooth Operator peanut butter

1 can (14 ounces) light coconut milk

1/2 pound rice noodles, cooked

There is nothing quite like this authentic Thai-style soup—it's sweet and tart, rich and savory, and light and creamy all at the same time. It's a great starter course and could easily be a meal in itself.

MAKES 6 SERVINGS

1. In a large stockpot, heat the oil and sauté the onion and garlic over medium heat until translucent.

2. Add the stock, tofu, mushrooms, lime juice, lemongrass, ginger, and bay leaves and simmer for 30 minutes.

3. Add the peanut butter and coconut milk and stir until well combined. Simmer an additional 10 minutes, stirring every few minutes.

4. Remove the bay leaves from the soup. Divide the cooked rice noodles into 6 bowls, ladle the soup over the noodles, and serve.

Did You Know?

Nobody consumes as much peanut butter as Americans; however, it is also popular in Canada, Holland, England, Germany, and Saudi Arabia. It is gaining popularity throughout Eastern Europe.

Vegetarian Masaman Curry

2 tablespoons peanut, corn, or canola oil

1 large yellow onion, chopped

3 cloves garlic, minced

1 package (14 ounces) extra-firm tofu, cut into 1-inch cubes

2 cups vegetable stock

1 can (14 ounces) light coconut milk

$^1/_2$ cup The Heat Is On peanut butter (see p. 13)

$^1/_2$ teaspoon sea salt

$^1/_4$ teaspoon black pepper, freshly ground

4 medium-sized carrots, peeled and cut into 1-inch pieces

3 medium-sized potatoes, peeled and cut into 1-inch pieces

1 cup frozen peas

3 tablespoons chopped, fresh basil

There are two things people say to me after I give them this recipe. The first is that it's so easy to prepare. The second is that there's no curry powder or curry paste in the recipe! The spicy peanut butter serves as the curry paste here, and contrary to popular belief, not all curries have curry powder in them. Serve over warm basmati rice with cool plain yogurt and sweet mango chutney on the side.

MAKES 4 SERVINGS

1. Place a large skillet over medium heat and add the oil, swirling to coat the bottom of the pan. Add the onion, garlic, and tofu and sauté until the tofu is slightly browned, the onions and garlic have lost most of their color, and any liquid in the pan is slightly sweet, about 5 to 7 minutes.

2. Meanwhile, combine the vegetable stock and coconut milk in a large saucepan and bring to a simmer. Add the peanut butter, salt, and pepper and stir until well incorporated. Add the carrots and potatoes and simmer until they're just about fully cooked, about 15 minutes, depending on the size of the vegetables. Add the tofu and onion mixture to the curry, along with the frozen peas. Continue to simmer on low heat for about 5 minutes, or until all of the vegetables are fully cooked.

3. Stir in the basil just before serving.

Peanut Butter–Marshmallow Sweet Potatoes

4 large sweet potatoes, peeled and sliced into large pieces

¹/₃ cup (²/₃ stick) **unsalted butter**

¹/₂ cup maple syrup

¹/₃ cup Smooth Operator peanut butter

1 teaspoon ground cinnamon

¹/₂ teaspoon salt

1 cup mini marshmallows

For me, autumn is all about the harvest—the flavors and colors are so bright and rich, I can't wait to get to work in the kitchen. This is a satisfying dish to serve on a crisp, cool night and will certainly perk up any traditional Thanksgiving feast.

MAKES 6 SERVINGS

1. Preheat the oven to 350°F.

2. Boil or steam the sweet potatoes until soft.

3. Place the cooked sweet potatoes in a medium saucepan. Add the butter, maple syrup, peanut butter, cinnamon, and salt. Cook over low heat for 5 minutes, mashing the ingredients together to create a uniform consistency.

4. Transfer the potato mixture to an 8-inch square ovenproof serving dish and top with the mini marshmallows. Bake for about 5 minutes, or until the marshmallows start to melt and lightly brown. Serve immediately.

PEANUT BUTTER FROM THE PAST

PEANUT BUTTER WAS ONE OF HEINZ'S
ORIGINAL 57 VARIETIES.

Big Green Salad with Grilled Chicken and Zesty Peanut Butter Vinaigrette

6 cups of salad greens, torn or coarsely chopped

1 large ripe tomato, chopped

1 red onion, coarsely chopped

1 portabella mushroom cap, chopped

1 cucumber, thinly sliced

Zesty Peanut Butter Vinaigrette (recipe follows)

2 grilled boneless, skinless chicken breasts, cut into strips

2 hard-boiled eggs, quartered

1/2 cup roasted, salted peanuts, coarsely chopped

This healthful salad is full of protein and is hearty enough for dinner. The Zesty Peanut Butter Vinaigrette is sweet, tart, and just a little bit spicy, the perfect dressing to tie together all the elements of the salad.

MAKES 2 SERVINGS

1. Place the greens in a large salad bowl. Add the tomato, onion, mushroom, and cucumber. Pour 1/2 cup of the vinaigrette over the vegetables and toss.

2. Divide the salad into two large serving bowls. Lay half the chicken and egg on top of each salad. Sprinkle the peanuts on top and serve.

Zesty Peanut Butter Vinaigrette

MAKES ABOUT 1 CUP

Combine the olive oil, vinegar, and peanut butter in a blender and pulse for 1 minute. Keep refrigerated until just before using.

1/3 cup olive oil

1/2 cup rice vinegar

2 tablespoons The Heat Is On peanut butter (see p. 13)

Cold Sesame Noodles

1 pound spaghetti

1 red bell pepper, julienned

1 large cucumber, julienned

1 scallion, chopped

2 tablespoons chopped fresh mint

1/4 cup chopped fresh cilantro

2/3 cup Smooth Operator peanut butter

1 small yellow onion, chopped

3 cloves garlic

1 1/2 tablespoons grated fresh ginger

1/3 cup rice vinegar

1/3 cup soy sauce

3 tablespoons freshly squeezed lime juice

3 tablespoons toasted sesame oil

One of my favorite things to order at any Chinese restaurant is Cold Sesame Noodles, and this is the way many people first encounter peanut butter in Asian cooking. This dish is great to serve at dinner as either a starter or a side dish, or try combining it with some mixed greens for a light lunch. You can even prepare it in advance and store it in the refrigerator for up to 3 days.

MAKES 6 SERVINGS

1. Cook the spaghetti according to the directions on the package. Drain and rinse with cold water.

2. In a large bowl, combine the spaghetti with the bell pepper, cucumber, scallion, mint, and cilantro.

3. In a blender, purée the peanut butter, onion, garlic, ginger, vinegar, soy sauce, lime juice, and sesame oil until smooth.

4. Toss the sauce over the pasta and vegetables. Refrigerate for 1 hour before serving for optimum flavor. Serve chilled or at room temperature.

Did You Know?

Folks on the East Coast prefer smooth peanut butter, while those on the West Coast prefer crunchy.

chapter 5
desserts, cakes, pies & pastries

Four-Layer Peanut Butter–Honey Cake

5 cups flour

2 tablespoons baking powder

2 teaspoons ground cinnamon

1 1/2 teaspoons salt

2 cups sugar

2 cups honey

1 cup canola or vegetable oil

1 tablespoon vanilla extract

8 large eggs

2 cups whole milk

Peanut Butter Frosting (recipe follows)

---

1 1/4 cups (2 1/2 sticks) unsalted butter, softened

1/4 cup Smooth Operator peanut butter

5 cups confectioners' sugar

1/2 teaspoon salt

1/4 cup plus 1 tablespoon whole milk

Everybody has a "honey," someone special who's worth going that extra mile for. Prepare this impressive treat for the honey in your life.

MAKES 12 SERVINGS

1. Preheat the oven to 350°F. Butter the bottom and sides of two 10-inch round cake pans. Dust the pans with flour and tap out the excess.

2. In a large bowl, sift together the flour, baking powder, cinnamon, and salt. Set aside.

3. In a separate large bowl, use an electric mixer to combine the sugar, honey, oil, and vanilla. Continue mixing and add the eggs one at a time, and then the milk. Add the dry ingredients, 1/2 cup at a time, and continue mixing until smooth.

4. Divide the batter evenly between the pans. Bake the cakes for 40 to 50 minutes, or until an inserted toothpick comes out clean. Allow the cakes to cool in the pans on a cooling rack for 30 minutes and then turn out onto a wire rack to cool completely before proceeding to the next step.

5. Using a serrated knife, trim the cakes so the tops are level. Slice each layer in half horizontally to make four rounds. Place a layer on a cake stand or serving dish, and build the cake using 3/4 cup of the Peanut Butter Frosting between each layer. Spread the remaining icing over the top and sides. Serve the cake within 2 to 3 hours after frosting, or refrigerate and bring to room temperature before serving.

Peanut Butter Frosting

MAKES 4 CUPS

In a large mixing bowl, use an electric mixer to whip the butter and peanut butter together. Add the confectioners' sugar, salt, and then the milk. Add additional tablespoons of milk or sugar to loosen or tighten the icing, respectively. For best results, use immediately.

Peanut Butter–Caramel Cheesecake

Everybody loves cheesecake. And cheesecake with peanut butter and caramel—well that's a no-brainer. This cool and creamy dessert is so tempting, you'd better invite some friends over right away so you don't eat it all yourself!

MAKES 8 SERVINGS

FOR THE CRUST

1 1/2 **cups graham cracker crumbs**

3 tablespoons light **brown sugar**

1/3 **cup** (2/3 stick) **unsalted butter**, melted

FOR THE FILLING

3 **packages** (8 ounces each) **cream cheese**, softened

3/4 **cup sour cream**

1 **teaspoon vanilla extract**

1 **cup granulated sugar**

3 **large eggs**

12 **individual caramels**, unwrapped

1/2 **cup sweetened condensed milk**

1 **cup Smooth Operator peanut butter**

1. Preheat the oven to 325°F. Butter the bottom and sides of a 9-inch springform pan.

2. To make the crust, mix the graham cracker crumbs, brown sugar, and butter in a bowl until well combined. Firmly pat the crust into the bottom of the prepared pan.

3. To make the filling, use an electric mixer to combine the cream cheese, sour cream, vanilla, and granulated sugar in a large bowl. Add the eggs, one at a time, and then gently pour the filling over the crust.

4. In a medium saucepan over low heat, combine the caramels, condensed milk, peanut butter, and 3/4 cup of water, stirring constantly until completely melted. Drizzle the peanut butter mixture over the cheesecake and use a butter knife to marbleize the topping.

5. Bake on the top rack of the oven for 50 to 60 minutes, or until an inserted toothpick comes out clean. Put a pan full of water on the bottom rack of the oven during baking to help create a moist cake. Allow the cheesecake to cool for 1 hour before removing from the pan, then refrigerate immediately.

Nutty Moments in History

Astronaut Alan B. Shepard brought a peanut with him to the moon.

Peanut Butter and Pineapple Upside-Down Cake

1 cup (2 sticks) **unsalted butter**

²/3 **cup light brown sugar,** packed

1 can (20 ounces) **pineapple rings,** drained, with 3 tablespoons juice reserved

¹/2 **cup maraschino cherries,** drained

1 cup flour, sifted

1 ¹/2 teaspoons baking powder

¹/2 **teaspoon salt**

³/4 **cup granulated sugar**

1 tablespoon vanilla extract

¹/2 **cup whole milk**

2 large eggs

1 cup Smooth Operator peanut butter

Whipped cream or vanilla ice cream, for serving

Mr. Bixby was a friend of my family who used to bake his mother's recipe for pineapple upside-down cake once a year. He was a peanut butter lover, too, and one day we thought to combine the two. The pineapple and cherries are a sweet foil to the peanut butter that makes this cake so rich. This cake is also easy to prepare—you get a great topping for your cake without the work of preparing and applying frosting.

MAKES 10 SERVINGS

1. Preheat the oven to 350°F.

2. In a large, ovenproof skillet at least 2 inches deep, combine ³/4 cup of the butter with the brown sugar over low heat, stirring constantly until the brown sugar is dissolved. Remove from the heat and place a pineapple ring in the center of the skillet. Place the additional pineapple rings in a circle around the center pineapple ring. Place a cherry in the center of each ring and set aside.

3. In a large bowl, sift together the flour, baking powder, and salt and set aside. In a separate large bowl, use an electric mixer to cream the remaining ¹/4 cup butter, the granulated sugar, and the vanilla. Add the milk, the 3 tablespoons reserved pineapple juice, and the eggs, one at a time, mixing well after each addition. Then add the peanut butter, beating until the mixture is well combined. Stir in the flour mixture. Do not overmix.

4. Carefully grease the sides of the skillet. Pour the batter into the skillet and use a spatula to gently spread the batter to evenly cover the pan. Bake 40 to 45 minutes, or until the center of the cake springs back lightly when touched. Remove from the oven and allow the cake to cool in the pan for 15 minutes. Loosen the edges of the cake with a spatula and turn the cake out onto a serving plate. Serve with whipped cream or vanilla ice cream.

Chocolate–Peanut Butter Flourless Cake

1 cup (2 sticks) **unsalted butter**

2 cups Dark Chocolate Dreams peanut butter (see p. 13)

1 bag (12 ounces) **semisweet chocolate chips**

8 large eggs

Vanilla ice cream, for serving

Did You Know?

November is Peanut Butter Lover's Month; March is National Peanut Month.

Flourless chocolate cake is one of those desserts everybody loves to order at restaurants but seems too hard to prepare at home. Surprise!—this is really one of the easiest things in the world to bake, and a very impressive final course to serve to guests.

MAKES 10 SERVINGS

1. Preheat the oven to 350°F. Butter the bottom and sides of 10-inch round cake pan. Dust the pan with flour and tap out excess.

2. Make a double boiler by filling a medium-sized saucepan halfway with water and placing a large glass bowl on top of the pan. Bring the water to a boil and add the butter and peanut butter to the bowl. Mix until well incorporated and turn off the heat. Add the chocolate chips and stir until the chocolate is completely melted. Transfer the mixture to a fresh bowl.

3. In a separate large bowl, use an electric mixer to whisk the eggs for 3 to 5 minutes, until their volume doubles. Fold one-third of the whipped eggs into the chocolate–peanut butter mixture and gradually add the rest of the eggs until the mixture is well combined.

4. Pour the mixture into the prepared cake pan and bake for 15 to 20 minutes. The center of the cake will be soft and gooey. Serve immediately with vanilla ice cream.

Peanut Butter and Strawberry Shortcakes

FOR THE SHORTCAKES

2 ¹/₂ cups flour

¹/₂ cup sugar

3 ¹/₂ teaspoons baking powder

¹/₂ teaspoon salt

¹/₂ cup (1 stick) unsalted butter, chilled

2 large eggs

¹/₂ cup light cream

FOR THE STRAWBERRIES

2 pints strawberries, hulled and quartered lengthwise

¹/₃ cup sugar

FOR THE WHIPPED CREAM

2 cups heavy cream

1 cup Smooth Operator peanut butter

1 cup whole milk

1 teaspoon vanilla extract

¹/₂ cup confectioners' sugar

If you've ever been lucky enough to go strawberry picking in early summer, you know how intoxicating the aroma of the freshest strawberries can be. After one such berry-picking trip, I was inspired to introduce peanut butter into this classic summertime treat, and I think you'll agree it's a winner.

MAKES 6 SERVINGS

1. Preheat the oven to 350°F. Cover a cookie sheet with parchment paper.

2. To make the shortcakes, in a large bowl, sift together the flour, sugar, baking powder, and salt. Using a pastry blender or two knives, cut the butter into the flour mixture until it resembles coarse meal.

3. In another large bowl, whisk together the eggs and light cream. Stir into the flour mixture until just combined.

4. Turn out the dough onto a lightly floured work surface. Dust it lightly with flour, then gently press the dough to a ¹/₂-inch thickness. Cut into shortcakes using a 3-inch biscuit cutter, reworking the scraps to make a total of 6. Transfer the shortcakes to the prepared cookie sheet. Bake for 20 minutes, or until golden brown. Transfer the cakes to a wire rack and cool for at least 15 to 20 minutes.

5. Meanwhile, prepare the strawberries. Place them in a large bowl and sprinkle the sugar on top. Toss the strawberries with the sugar, bruising the berries slightly. Cover and refrigerate for 1 to 2 hours.

6. To prepare the whipped cream, place the heavy cream in a large bowl and use an electric mixer to whip the cream until stiff peaks form. In a blender, combine the peanut butter, milk, vanilla, and confectioners' sugar and pulse until well combined. Fold the peanut butter mixture into the whipped cream and refrigerate until serving.

7. To assemble the cakes, slice each shortcake in half horizontally and top with strawberries and the whipped cream. Replace the top half of the shortcake and serve immediately.

Peanut Butter Tiramisu

3 large eggs, separated

1 cup espresso or strong, black coffee, chilled

1/2 cup plus a pinch of sugar

2 tablespoons cognac

1 cup Smooth Operator peanut butter

8 ounces mascarpone cheese

20 toasted ladyfinger cookies

2 tablespoons unsweetened cocoa powder

Tiramisu is an Italian dessert whose name means "pick-me-up," and the combination of sugar and espresso in this recipe certainly is eye-opening. This is a rich, elegant dessert that is made even more tasty with the addition of peanut butter to the cream layers. It's perfect to serve after a late summer supper.

MAKES 5 SERVINGS

1. In a large bowl, use an electric mixer to combine the egg yolks, 1 tablespoon of the espresso, the 1/2 cup sugar, the cognac, and the peanut butter. Add the mascarpone cheese and continue mixing until smooth.

2. In another large bowl, combine the egg whites and a pinch of sugar. With clean beaters, whip the egg whites until the mixture forms stiff peaks. Gently fold the beaten egg whites into the mascarpone mixture.

3. Pour the remaining espresso into a shallow bowl and dip 10 of the ladyfingers into the coffee, arranging them on the bottom of a 9 x 13-inch glass baking dish. Spread half of the mascarpone mixture on top of the ladyfingers and sprinkle with half of the cocoa. Dip the remaining ladyfingers in the espresso, layer them on top of the cocoa-covered mascarpone mixture, and top with the remaining mascarpone mixture. Sprinkle with the remaining cocoa and refrigerate for at least 1 hour before serving.

Notes: Store-bought ladyfingers are usually pretoasted and ready to soak up the espresso in this recipe. If you happen to buy them fresh and they are soft and spongy, toast them in the oven for a few minutes. Allow them to cool completely before dipping them in the espresso.

• This recipe contains raw eggs, which can carry salmonella bacteria. This recipe can also be prepared using pasteurized eggs and egg whites, which can be found at most grocery stores.

Chocolate–Peanut Butter Pie

FOR THE CRUST

2 cups crushed chocolate wafer cookies

1/4 cup (1/2 stick) unsalted butter, melted

1/2 cup (1 stick) unsalted butter

1/2 cup semisweet chocolate chips

FOR THE FILLING

1 cup heavy cream

1/2 cup (4 ounces) cream cheese

3/4 cup Smooth Operator peanut butter

1/2 cup confectioners' sugar

2 tablespoons whole milk

2 tablespoons vanilla extract

FOR THE TOPPING

1/4 cup semisweet chocolate chips

1/4 cup peanut butter chips

3 tablespoons roasted, salted peanuts, coarsely chopped

Whipped cream, for garnish

This is a favorite dessert at Peanut Butter & Co. Customers have told us they've driven more than a hundred miles for a slice of our signature chocolate–peanut butter pie. If well wrapped, it will keep in the freezer for up to 2 months.

MAKES 6 SERVINGS

1. To make the crust, place the crushed chocolate wafer cookies in a 10-inch glass pie plate. Add the 1/4 cup melted butter and toss with a fork until all the crumbs are coated. Use your hands to press the crust onto the bottom and sides of the pie plate. Refrigerate for 10 minutes to set.

2. Make a double boiler by filling a medium-sized saucepan halfway with water and placing a large glass bowl on top of the pan. Bring the water to a boil and then turn off the heat. Add the 1/2 cup butter and chocolate chips and stir until the chocolate is completely melted. Gently pour the chocolate mixture into the pie shell and tilt to coat the bottom evenly.

3. To make the filling, in a medium bowl, use an electric mixer to whip the cream until it is firm. For best results, start out with very cold cream. Beat at low speed for about 30 seconds, then turn the mixer speed to high, continuing to beat until the cream is firm and holds a peak. Place the cream in the refrigerator.

4. In a large mixing bowl, use an electric mixer to combine the cream cheese, peanut butter, confectioners' sugar, milk, and vanilla. Beat for about 30 seconds, or until well combined. Remove the whipped cream from the refrigerator and carefully fold it into the peanut butter mixture.

5. To assemble the pie, pour the filling into the prepared pie crust, spreading evenly. Top with the chocolate chips, peanut butter chips, and peanuts. Cover with plastic wrap and place the pie in the freezer for about 1 hour to set.

6. About 1 hour before you plan to serve, transfer the pie from the freezer to the refrigerator. At serving time, cut the pie into slices and garnish each slice with a dollop of whipped cream.

Peanut Butter Pumpkin Pie

FOR THE CRUST

1 1/4 cups all-purpose flour

1 teaspoon sugar

1/2 teaspoon salt

1/2 cup (1 stick) **unsalted butter,** diced and chilled

1 large egg, beaten and chilled

FOR THE FILLING

3/4 cup sugar

1 teaspoon ground cinnamon

1/2 teaspoon freshly grated nutmeg

1/2 teaspoon ground ginger

1/2 teaspoon salt

2 large eggs

1 can (15 ounces) unsweetened pumpkin purée

1/2 cup Smooth Operator peanut butter

1 can (12 ounces) evaporated milk

Vanilla ice cream or whipped cream, for serving

Come Thanksgiving in America, everybody's eating pumpkin pie, and it seems we just can't get enough of the stuff. Try this recipe, which combines peanut butter with pumpkin.

MAKES 8 SERVINGS

1. Preheat the oven to 420°F.

2. To make the crust, sift together the flour, sugar, and salt in a large mixing bowl. Using a pastry blender or two knives, cut the butter into the flour mixture until it resembles coarse meal. Add the egg and mix gently. If the dough is too dry, add ice water, 1/2 teaspoon at a time, until it becomes workable. Transfer the dough to a sheet of plastic wrap and press into a disk. Cover with another sheet of plastic wrap and refrigerate for 1 hour.

3. Turn the dough out onto a lightly floured surface, and use a rolling pin to roll the dough into a 12-inch circle about 1/8 inch thick. Transfer the dough to a 9-inch pie pan. Use your fingers to flute the edges, trimming any excess. Refrigerate for 30 minutes before filling.

4. Combine the sugar, cinnamon, nutmeg, ginger, and salt in a small bowl and set aside.

5. In a large bowl, use an electric mixer to beat the eggs, then add the pumpkin and peanut butter, mixing until smooth. Continue to mix while you add the dry ingredients, then add the evaporated milk and mix until well combined.

6. Gently pour the pumpkin mixture into the pie shell and bake on the top rack of the oven for 15 minutes. Reduce the oven temperature to 350°F and bake for an additional 40 to 50 minutes, or until a knife inserted into the center of the pie comes out clean. Cool for at least 2 hours before serving. Serve with vanilla ice cream or whipped cream.

Maple–Peanut Butter Mousse

2/3 cup **Smooth Operator peanut butter**

2/3 cup **maple syrup**

1 cup **whole milk**

2 cups **heavy cream**

Roasted peanuts, for garnish

Shaved chocolate, for garnish

The word mousse *is French for "frothy," and in English, it has come to mean a light and fluffy, usually sweet, dish. The next time you're in the mood for something light and fluffy, sweet and nutty, try this Maple–Peanut Butter Mousse. It's perfect when you're looking for a sweet way to end a meal with something that's not too heavy.*

MAKES 6 SERVINGS

1. In a blender, whip together the peanut butter, maple syrup, and milk.

2. In a large bowl, use an electric mixer to whip the cream until it doubles in volume and forms stiff peaks. Fold the peanut butter mixture into the cream and pour into footed parfait or dessert dishes.

3. Refrigerate for at least 2 hours to set. Sprinkle with roasted peanuts or shaved chocolate just before serving.

Peanut Butter Parfait

This no-bake recipe is quick and easy to prepare, with virtually no cleanup. It's just about as healthful as can be and is as satisfying in the morning for breakfast as it is in the evening for dessert.

1 **large ripe banana,** peeled and cut into 1/2-inch slices

2 tablespoons **Smooth Operator peanut butter**

2 tablespoons **Grape Nuts® cereal**

1 container (8 ounces) **vanilla yogurt**

2 tablespoons **honey**

MAKES 1 SERVING

1. Place the banana slices in a footed parfait or dessert glass. Spoon the peanut butter over the bananas and then sprinkle the Grape Nuts on top of the peanut butter.

2. Top with the yogurt and drizzle with the honey. Serve immediately.

Chocolate–Peanut Butter Bread Pudding

12 slices brioche or challah, at least 1 day old

1 1/2 cups Dark Chocolate Dreams peanut butter (see p. 13)

2 cups light cream

1/4 teaspoon salt

1 teaspoon vanilla extract

1 cup sugar

3 large eggs

When I think comfort food, I think bread pudding, and I think of this dessert as the ultimate bread pudding for the peanut butter and chocolate lover. This is the perfect way to end a meal on a cold wintry day, and the leftovers are great the following day! Serve warm with vanilla ice cream.

MAKES 6 SERVINGS

1. Preheat the oven to 350°F. Grease an 8-inch square baking dish.

2. Make 6 sandwiches with the bread and peanut butter using 1/4 cup of peanut butter in each. Cut each sandwich into 6 to 8 pieces. Pile the sandwich pieces into the prepared baking dish.

3. In a small saucepan, combine the cream, salt, and vanilla and cook over medium heat until hot.

4. In a large bowl, whisk together the sugar and eggs. Slowly add the hot cream mixture, stirring constantly to make sure the eggs do not cook. Pour the mixture over the bread and cover the dish with aluminum foil. Bake on the center rack of the oven for 30 to 40 minutes, removing the foil after about 20 minutes. The finished pudding will be golden brown on top. Allow the pudding to rest for at least 10 minutes before serving.

NEAT-O!

Americans eat enough peanut butter in a year to make more than 10 billion peanut butter and jelly sandwiches.

Peanut Butter Rice Pudding

4 cups light cream

1 cup whole milk

3/4 cup sugar

1/2 tablespoon vanilla extract

1/2 teaspoon ground cinnamon

Pinch of salt

1 cup Arborio rice

1/2 cup golden raisins

1/2 cup diced dried apricots

1/2 cup Smooth Operator peanut butter

Whipped cream, for serving

Orange marmalade, for serving

Roasted, salted peanuts, chopped, for serving

Rice pudding is a traditional dessert in India and the Middle East that came to Europe through its colonies in those locales. The traditional recipes often contained dried fruits and nuts. While the rice pudding you grew up with may have been decidedly more plain, this jazzed-up version is actually pretty close to the way it was originally prepared hundreds of years ago. Fancy that!

MAKES 4 TO 6 SERVINGS

1. In a large stockpot with a lid, combine the cream, milk, sugar, vanilla, cinnamon, and salt over medium heat. Bring to a simmer and add the rice. Reduce the heat to low, cover, and cook, stirring frequently to prevent the rice from sticking to the bottom of the pot. Cook for 45 minutes, or until the rice is fully cooked. There will still be liquid in the pot.

2. Remove the pot from the heat and stir in the raisins, apricots, and peanut butter. Allow the mixture to cool to room temperature and then refrigerate for at least 3 hours.

3. Serve with a dollop of whipped cream, a spoonful of marmalade, and a sprinkling of chopped peanuts.

Did You Know?

Arachibutyrophobia (pronounced I-RA-KID-BU-TI-RO-PHO-BIA) is the fear of getting peanut butter stuck to the roof of your mouth.

Peanut Butter Ice Cream

6 egg yolks

3 cups heavy cream

1 cup whole milk

1 tablespoon vanilla extract

1 cup light brown sugar

1 cup Smooth Operator peanut butter

$^1/_2$ cup grated semisweet chocolate (optional)

I scream, you scream, we all scream for ice cream! This peanut butter ice cream is rich and creamy and tastier than most anything you can buy at the store, and today's electric ice cream makers make the preparation so much easier than in days of yore. Just think of all of the different things you can find to fold and swirl into it to make your own custom flavors!

MAKES 6 SERVINGS

1. Place the egg yolks in a small bowl. Whisk together and set aside.

2. In a medium saucepan, heat the cream, milk, vanilla, and brown sugar over low heat until the sugar is dissolved. Remove the pan from the heat and stir 2 tablespoons of the warm cream mixture into the beaten egg yolks. Slowly add the yolk mixture to the warm cream mixture, stirring constantly so the eggs don't cook. Return the cream mixture to the stove and cook over low heat for about 5 minutes, stirring constantly. Remove from the heat when the cream coats the back of a spoon. Pour the warm cream mixture through a sieve into a large bowl and refrigerate until cool.

3. Pour the chilled ice cream mixture into an ice cream maker and add the peanut butter. Freeze the ice cream according to the manufacturer's directions. Just before the machine is finished, add the grated chocolate if using. Transfer the ice cream to a freezer-safe container and freeze an additional 2 hours before serving.

PEANUT BUTTER FROM THE PAST

A VINTAGE DINER SIGN ADVERTISES THE HOUSE SPECIALTY, PEANUT BUTTER ICE CREAM.

Death by Peanut Butter™

1/2 cup Cap'n Crunch's
Peanut Butter Crunch®
cereal

3 scoops vanilla ice cream

2 tablespoons Smooth
Operator peanut butter

1/4 cup peanut butter chips

1/4 cup Reese's Pieces®

1/4 cup whipped cream

2 tablespoons store-
bought peanut butter
dessert sauce

This is the most popular dessert at Peanut Butter & Co. Sometimes I think people order it just so they can say the name. It's a big sundae, and it's great for sharing. Just don't eat it too fast—you might get brain freeze!

MAKES 1 SUNDAE

Place the cereal in the bottom of a serving dish. Add the ice cream, then the peanut butter, peanut butter chips, and Reese's Pieces. Top the sundae with whipped cream and finish with a drizzle of peanut butter sauce.

The Bananarama™

1 large ripe banana

3 scoops vanilla ice cream

1/4 cup Marshmallow Fluff

2 tablespoons Smooth
Operator peanut butter

3 graham cracker squares

1/4 cup whipped cream

2 tablespoons chocolate
sauce

One day a customer came into the shop and asked for a peanut butter banana split, which wasn't on the menu at the time. I thought about it for a minute and realized that it was the perfect opportunity to combine all sorts of flavors and textures. The sundae looked so good that another customer asked for one as well. It became a permanent menu item the very next day!

MAKES 1 SUNDAE

1. Slice the banana in half lengthwise, then cut each slice in half.

2. Place the banana in the bottom of a serving dish and add the ice cream, Marshmallow Fluff, and peanut butter. Position the graham cracker squares between the scoops of ice cream. Top the sundae with whipped cream and finish with a drizzle of chocolate sauce.

Peanut Butter–Berry Crumble

2 tablespoons cornstarch

1 tablespoon lemon juice

1 cup granulated sugar

1 cup blueberries

1 cup raspberries

1 cup strawberries

1 cup blackberries

1 1/2 cups rolled oats

1/2 cup flour

2/3 cup light brown sugar

1/2 teaspoon ground cinnamon

1/2 teaspoon salt

1/2 cup (1 stick) **unsalted butter,** cut into 1/2-inch cubes

1/2 cup Smooth Operator peanut butter

Vanilla ice cream, for serving

A crumble is a British dessert traditionally made with fresh berries that are baked with a rich crumb topping. While fresh berries are always best, you can use frozen berries and prepare this satisfying dessert any time of year.

MAKES 6 SERVINGS

1. Preheat the oven to 350°F.

2. In a large bowl, combine the cornstarch, lemon juice, and 1/4 cup cold water. Stir until the cornstarch is completely dissolved. Add the granulated sugar, blueberries, raspberries, strawberries, and blackberries, and mix gently so as to not bruise the fruit. Place the fruit mixture in an 11 x 7-inch baking dish.

3. In a separate medium bowl, combine the rolled oats, flour, brown sugar, cinnamon, and salt. Cut in the butter and peanut butter and stir until the mixture is the consistency of coarse meal. Sprinkle on top of the fruit mixture and bake for 20 minutes, or until the top is golden brown. Serve warm with vanilla ice cream.

NEAT-O!

Peanut butter is the leading use of peanuts in the United States.

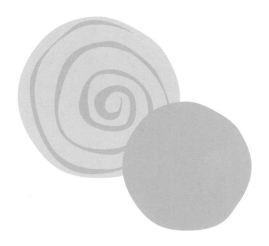

Peanut Butter & Co. Apple Strudel

¹/₂ cup (1 stick) unsalted butter

5 sheets of phyllo dough (13 x 18 inches)

3 medium-sized Granny Smith apples, peeled, cored, and cut into bite-size pieces

1³/₄ cups Cinnamon Raisin Swirl peanut butter (see p. 13)

NEAT-O!

Although peanut butter is considered a kid's food, adults actually eat more peanut butter than kids each year.

Strudel is a traditional Viennese dessert made with apples, nuts, cinnamon, and raisins. This sounds like a job for our Cinnamon Raisin Swirl peanut butter! This recipe is especially fun to prepare in autumn, when there are lots of fresh apples around. Serve this satisfying dessert warm with vanilla ice cream.

MAKES 8 SERVINGS

1. Preheat the oven to 350°F.

2. Clarify the butter by placing it in a small saucepan over low heat. After the butter melts completely, you'll notice the white foamy solids rising to the top. Spoon out the solids so that only a clear liquid remains.

3. Place one sheet of phyllo dough on a nonstick cookie sheet. Brush with clarified butter and top with another sheet of phyllo dough. Repeat the process with the remaining sheets of phyllo dough. Do not spread butter on the top sheet.

4. In a medium bowl, combine the apples and peanut butter. Spoon the mixture in a strip 3 to 3¹/₂ inches wide down the center of the phyllo dough, leaving a 2-inch border at the ends.

5. Fold up the ends of the phyllo dough and brush with butter. Fold one side of the phyllo dough over, and then the other, using the butter as glue to seal the seams. Carefully turn the strudel over and brush the remaining butter on top of the pastry. Score the top of the strudel with diagonal cuts.

6. Bake the strudel for 15 to 20 minutes, or until golden brown. Remove from the oven and allow to cool for at least 10 minutes before slicing.

Peanut Butter–Banana Fritters

1 1/2 **cups flour**

2 **teaspoons baking powder**

1/4 **teaspoon salt**

1 **cup whole milk**

2 **large eggs,** lightly beaten

1/2 **cup light brown sugar**

3/4 **cup Smooth Operator peanut butter**

3 **large bananas,** chopped

1 **to** 2 **cups light vegetable oil,** such as canola oil

Confectioners' sugar

The mother of a friend of mine used to make these banana fritters for the neighborhood kids. They take a little time to prepare, and we'd sit around their kitchen table playfully complaining about how hungry we were. She'd prepare the whole batch so we'd all get to eat at once, and just before we were hysterical with anticipation, she'd turn to us and say, "Don't go all a-twitter, here's your banana fritter!" It seems silly now, but back then it used to crack us up. Good luck holding your friends or family at bay while you prepare this special treat.

MAKES 2 DOZEN FRITTERS

1. In a large mixing bowl, sift together the flour, baking powder, and salt.

2. In a blender, mix together the milk, eggs, brown sugar, and peanut butter. Fold the wet ingredients into the dry, and when well incorporated, fold in the chopped bananas. Place the batter in the refrigerator for 10 minutes.

3. Fill the bottom of a large skillet with 1 to 2 inches of the vegetable oil and place over medium heat for 2 to 3 minutes, or until a small drop of batter floats when placed in the oil.

4. Remove the batter from the refrigerator. Carefully drop the batter into the hot oil 1/3 cup at a time. Fry until golden brown, about 3 to 5 minutes on each side. Place the fritters on paper towels to absorb any excess oil and serve warm, dusted with confectioners' sugar.

Poached Pears with Dark Chocolate–Peanut Butter Sauce

1/4 cup sugar

1 teaspoon lemon juice

4 large Bosc pears, peeled, cored, and sliced in half lengthwise

Dark Chocolate–Peanut Butter Sauce (recipe follows)

1/4 cup heavy cream

2 tablespoons unsalted butter

2 tablespoons sugar

1/2 cup Dark Chocolate Dreams peanut butter (see p. 13)

Don't let the name fool you. This might sound like a fancy recipe—the kind you'd only eat at a fancy restaurant—but it's actually easy to prepare and something the whole family will enjoy. The sweet, mellow flavor of the pears is a great match for the rich Dark Chocolate–Peanut Butter Sauce.

MAKES 4 SERVINGS

1. Fill a large pot with 2 quarts of water and add the sugar and lemon juice. Bring the water to a simmer and add the pears. Cook for about 15 minutes, then let the pears cool in the water for another 15 minutes.

2. Place 2 pear halves on a plate and ladle 1/4 cup of the Dark Chocolate–Peanut Butter Sauce over the fruit. Repeat with remaining pear halves.

Dark Chocolate–Peanut Butter Sauce

MAKES ABOUT 1 CUP

In a small saucepan, heat the cream, butter, and sugar. Whisk in the peanut butter and simmer for 5 minutes, or until the sugar is dissolved, whisking constantly. Remove from the heat and allow to cool for 5 minutes before serving.

Peanut Butter Brittle

3 cups sugar

1 cup light corn syrup

1/2 teaspoon salt

4 cups roasted, salted peanuts

2 cups Smooth Operator peanut butter

2 tablespoons unsalted butter

1 teaspoon vanilla extract

2 teaspoons baking soda

Peanut Butter Brittle makes a great holiday gift. Try making this with The Heat Is On peanut butter (see p. 13) for a special treat for your favorite chile-head.

MAKES ABOUT 2 POUNDS

1. Lightly butter two 11 x 17-inch cookie sheets.

2. Combine the sugar, corn syrup, salt, and 1/2 cup water in a large saucepan over high heat and bring to a rolling boil. Add the peanuts and reduce the heat to medium, stirring constantly.

3. When the mixture reaches the hard-crack stage, about 300°F (use a candy thermometer to measure the temperature), remove the pan from the heat. Add the peanut butter, butter, and vanilla, and then the baking soda, stirring constantly. When you add the baking soda, the mixture will increase in volume dramatically.

4. Pour the mixture onto the prepared baking sheets, spreading to a 1/4-inch thickness. Allow to cool for 1 to 2 hours. Break the candy into large pieces and store in an airtight container.

Did You Know?

Four of the top ten candy bars manufactured in the United States contain peanuts or peanut butter.

PEANUT BUTTER BUCKEYES (P. 105), PEANUT BUTTER BRITTLE, AND PEANUT BUTTER FUDGE (P. 104)

Peanut Butter Fudge

5 cups (2 pounds) **firmly packed light brown sugar**

1¼ cups whole milk

1 tablespoon vanilla extract

½ teaspoon salt

¼ cup (½ stick) **unsalted butter**

1 cup Smooth Operator peanut butter

PEANUT BUTTER FROM THE PAST

IN THE 1970s, PEANUT FARMERS PROMOTED PEANUT BUTTER IN THE PSYCHEDELIC STYLE OF THE DAY.

No one really knows who invented fudge, but one popular story is that in 1886, a student at Vassar College (my alma mater) was sent some fudge by a cousin in Baltimore. It was such a hit in the dorm that she shared the recipe with her classmates. Two years later, Miss Emelyn Battersby Hartridge is reported to have made 30 pounds of the tasty treat for a fundraising event at the college. Word of the new confection spread to the other Seven Sisters (prestigious all-female colleges of the time), and no doubt those savvy Vassar girls made presents of homemade fudge to their Ivy League boyfriends studying at Harvard, Columbia, and Yale. Treat the peanut butter lover in your life to something special with a gift of this homemade peanut butter fudge.

MAKES ABOUT 36 PIECES

1. In a large saucepan over medium heat, combine the brown sugar, milk, vanilla, and salt and stir until the sugar is dissolved. Add the butter and cook to 238°F, soft-ball stage on a candy thermometer, stirring constantly.

2. Pour the fudge into a large heatproof bowl. Use an electric mixer to beat the fudge and immediately add the peanut butter. Continue beating just until the fudge loses its gloss and begins to stiffen. Quickly pour the fudge into an 8 x 8-inch square baking dish and allow to cool completely before cutting into 1½-inch squares.

Peanut Butter Buckeyes

1 1/2 cups **Smooth Operator peanut butter**

2 cups **confectioners' sugar**

1/2 cup **nonfat powdered milk**

1/2 **cup** (1 stick) **unsalted butter**

1 teaspoon **vanilla extract**

16 ounces **semisweet chocolate**

Buckeyes are traditionally homemade treats and are arguably the world's first peanut butter and chocolate candy. The buckeye candy gets its name because it looks like the nut of the buckeye tree.

MAKES 2 DOZEN BUCKEYES

1. Line a baking pan with waxed paper or parchment paper.

2. In a large bowl, mix the peanut butter, confectioners' sugar, powdered milk, margarine, and vanilla until semidry and crumbly.

3. Make a double boiler by filling a medium-sized saucepan halfway with water and placing a large glass bowl on top of the pan. Bring the water to a boil and then turn off the heat. Add the chocolate chips and stir until chocolate is completely melted.

4. Roll about a tablespoon of the peanut butter mixture in your hand to form a ball. Dip the ball into the melted chocolate using a toothpick or a small pair of tongs, leaving the top uncovered to resemble a buckeye. Place the ball on the prepared baking pan, and repeat with the remaining peanut butter mixture. Refrigerate until set, about 2 hours.

Did You Know?

Americans spend close to $1 billion each year on peanut butter.

Resources

We're proud that our products are carried by many of the country's top specialty food stores. Many of these stores are independently owned and operated and offer their customers unique shopping experiences.

Bristol Farms
Los Angeles, CA

Dean & DeLuca
New York, NY

Fox & Obel
Chicago, IL

Metropolitan Bakery
Philadelphia, PA

Norman Brothers Produce
Miami, FL

Rice Epicurean Markets
Houston, TX

A Southern Season
Chapel Hill, NC

Stew Leonard's
Norwalk, CT

Yum! Specialty Foods
San Francisco, CA

Zingerman's Deli
Ann Arbor, MI

Our products are also carried by a number of top supermarkets. Please look for our products in these stores as well, where they are usually stocked with the peanut butter or in the natural foods section:

Central Market
Texas

Food Emporium
New York Metro Area

Fresh Market
Southeast

Giant Supermarkets
Mid-Atlantic

Hannaford
New England and New York

Harmon's
Salt Lake City, UT

King Kullen
Long Island, NY

Kroger
National

Meijer
Midwest

Shaw's
New England

Stop + Shop
Connecticut, Massachusetts, New Hampshire, New York, New Jersy, and Rhode Island

Super Target
National

Ukrops
Virginia

Wegman's
Mid-Atlantic

Whole Foods
National

Acknowledgments

This book wouldn't have been possible without the support of so many people.

I am grateful to the teachers who encouraged me to express myself through writing. Mrs. Marks, Mrs. Seligsohn, Mrs. Kurtz, Mrs. Nehez, Dr. Kreider, Ms. Schroeder, Mr. Sassone, and Mr. Russell—thank you for your passion for teaching and all that you shared with me.

Starting a new business is fraught with numerous perils and pitfalls. Peanut Butter & Co. wouldn't have made it without the patience and flexibility of Francis Greenburger, Scott Klatsky, and Ben Feinstein—thank you for believing in our potential.

There are a number of New York food entrepreneurs who have advised and inspired me over the years—Abram Orwasher at Orwashers Bakery, Peter Singer at Betsy's Place, Pat Helding at Fatwitch Brownies, Peter Longo at Porto Rico Coffee, Stew Leonard Jr. at Stew Leonard's, Cindy Swenson at Start Button, and Chuck Hunt at the New York State Restaurant Association—thank you all for your friendship and counsel, and thank you, Dave Hovet, for teaching me so much about making peanut butter.

A number of companies supply us with the raw ingredients and distribution services we need to manufacture our products and get them to the consumer. Thank you Marvin Smith, Irwin Rappaport, Steve Spiegler, Jake Ritz, Tim Werkley, Niels Christensen, Michael Youmans, and Jim Curran for your dedication to high standards and ongoing professionalism.

As a young entrepreneur, I have been fortunate enough to have a number of people looking out for me. Anthony Williams and Michael Hagan, Brendan Marx, David Salkin, Dan Kornblatt, George Scholomiti, and Steve Zalben, thank you for watching my back.

Thank you, Jay Rosengarten, Charlie Moro, Wendy Green, and Doug Sumpter, as well as Stephen Deleo, Linda Hodnett, and Stewart Reich—you've helped me turn my little sandwich shop into a national brand.

Dee Dee Darden at the National Peanut Board, Leslie Wagner at the Peanut Advisory Board, Jeannette Anderson at the American Peanut Council, and Betsy Owens at Virginia-Carolina Peanut Promotions, thank you for your ongoing interest and support.

Pippa White designed our retro logo and the now-famous monkey that graces our jars—thank you, Pippa, and thank you, Joel Tractenberg for contributing exciting designs for new products.

David Black and Gary Morris, who believed in this book from the very beginning, and Melissa Wagner, Andrea Stephany, Jason Mitchell, Theresa Raffetto, Victoria Granof, and Barbara Fritz, thank you for helping me turn my passion for peanut butter into a fun-to-read pop-culture cookbook.

Thank you Jerry Seinfeld, for writing the foreword to this book, and for all of your and Jessica's support over the years.

There have been a number of good friends who have stood by me since the early days: Jason Klinman, who's seen me through thick and thin; Abby and Dave Rubin, fans from the start; Dan Shiffman, who believed in all of my wild and crazy ideas; Shira Hassan, my favorite vegan; Kyle Zvacek, who bussed a lot of tables and never complained once; and Ardythe Williams, my rock, my sounding board, my go-to gal.

Thank you, Greg Gale, my research whiz and recipe tester/taster extraordinaire, who has shown me a generosity of spirit beyond compare.

If you heard about Peanut Butter & Co. before picking up this book, it is most likely due to the public relations wizardry of Jennifer Niederhoffer. Thank you, Jennifer, for all that you do for me.

Thank you to everyone at 4 West, especially Lisa Lazarus and Sophia Ber, Palma Driscoll and Fabrice Trombert, and Bob Felner and Allison Levy.

Thanks to Mom, who made me that first peanut butter sandwich, and thanks to my brother Scott, who dipped his finger in the jar with me.

Marcie Polier, thank you for believing in Peanut Butter & Co. since the early days.

Bryan Bantry, thank you for making this and so many other things in my life possible.

Finally, I'd like to thank the entire Peanut Butter & Co. staff. It's your hard work that makes me look so good. Thanks for coming along on this nutty adventure with me.

Index

Page numbers in **bold** (for example, **73**)
indicate photographs.

Table of Equivalencies

For Volume:

U.S.	Metric
1/4 tsp	1.25 ml
1/2 tsp	2.5 ml
1 tsp	5 ml
1 tbsp (3 tsp)	15 ml
1 fl oz (2 tbsp)	30 ml
1/4 cup	60 ml
1/3 cup	80 ml
1/2 cup	120 ml
1 cup	240 ml
1 pint (2 cups)	480 ml
1 quart (2 pints)	960 ml
1 gallon (4 quarts)	3.84 liters

For Weight:

U.S.	Metric
1 oz	28 g
4 oz (1/4 lb)	113 g
8 oz (1/2 lb)	227 g
12 oz (3/4 lb)	340 g
16 oz (1 lb)	454 g
2.2 lb	1 kg

For Length:

Inches	Centimeters
1/4	0.65
1/2	1.25
1	2.50
2	5.00
3	7.50
4	10.0
5	12.5
6	15.0
7	17.5
8	20.5
9	23.0
10	25.5
12	30.5
15	38.0

Oven Temperature:

Degrees Fahrenheit	Degrees Centigrade	British Gas Marks
200	93	—
250	120	1/2
275	140	1
300	150	2
325	165	3
350	175	4
375	190	5
400	200	6
450	230	8
500	260	10